A PRACTICAL GUIDE FOR

GRIEF & LOSS

A PRACTICAL GUIDE FOR

GRIEF & LOSS

HOW TO FIND YOUR PATHWAY TO PEACE AND PURPOSE.

Diana Hutchison

Copyright © 2024 Diana Hutchison

All rights reserved. No part of this book may be used or reproduced by any means, graphic, electronic, or mechanical, including photocopying recording, taping or by any information storage retrieval system without written permission of the author/publisher except in the case of brief quotations embodied in critical articles and reviews.

 A catalogue record for this book is available from the National Library of Australia

The author of this book does not dispense medical advice or prescribe the use of any technique as a form of treatment, either directly or indirectly. The intent of the author is only to offer information of a general nature to help you in your quest for emotional and spiritual wellbeing. In the event you use any of the information in this book for yourself, which is your constitutional right, the author/publisher assume no responsibility for your actions. This book is not intended to be a substitute for the medical advice of a licensed physician. The reader should consult with their doctor in any matters relating to his/her health.

The material in this publication is of the nature of general comment only, and does not represent professional advice. It is not intended to provide specific guidance for particular circumstances and it should not be relied on as the basis for any decision to take action or not take action on any matter which it covers. Readers should obtain professional advice where appropriate, before making any such decision. To the maximum extent permitted by law, the author disclaims all responsibility and liability to any person, arising directly or indirectly from any person taking or not taking action based on the information in this publication.

Cover design: NGirl Design
Editor: Hari Teah

ACKNOWLEDGEMENT

This book was conceived and written on the land of the Kaurna People.

We acknowledge and respect their spiritual relationship with their land and country. We also acknowledge the Kaurna People as the custodians of the Adelaide Plains region and that their cultural and heritage beliefs are important through all time.

We acknowledge and pay our respects to the cultural authority of past, present and emerging leaders and acknowledge and listen to their voices and messages for greater cultural inclusion.

THE PRACTICAL GUIDE SERIES

The Practical Guide Series provides practical tips and guidance to empower you to apply self-transformational change within yourself and your life. The series overall explores self-change: internal and external, including changing habits, mindset, becoming who you want to be, and exploring how to heal yourself on all levels. Future books will go into more detail in self-healing and external healing. Each book is separate in its own right. Thus, they do not need to be read in any particular order.

> Previous books in this series:
> *by*
> **Diana Hutchison**
>
> - *A Practical Guide for Self Change*
> - *A Practical Guide for Young Adults: Consciously Create the Life You'll Love*

FREE DOWNLOADS

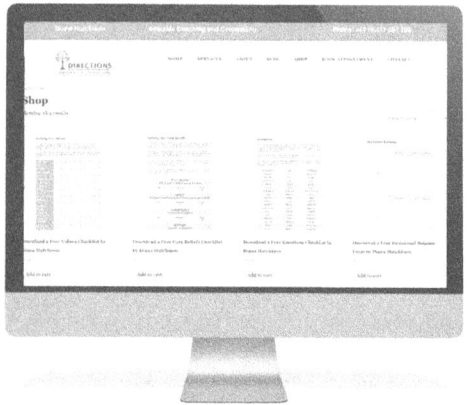

Grab your free downloads for self-assessment to accompany this book by visiting

www.dianahutchison.com/shop

CONTENTS

Foreword 1

Introduction 5

Chapter 1 Your Grief Journey 11

Chapter 2 Theories On Grief And Loss 31

Chapter 3 How Grief Expresses On All Levels 49

Chapter 4 Exploring Emotion 75

Chapter 5 The Process Of Grieving 97

Chapter 6 Secondary Losses 113

Chapter 7 Everyday Grief 127

Chapter 8 Where Are You Right Now? 145

Chapter 9 Finding Your Pathway To Self-Healing 159

Conclusion 165

References 169

FOREWORD

Guiding someone through grief and loss is an art that requires considerable skill. To help people find their way through one of the most challenging events in their life with and into a place where there is a renewed sense of peace and purpose is an even greater skill. This is why Diana Hutchison's expertise on the subject of grief and loss is so valuable to us all.

I was on my own pathway to peace and purpose when I first met Diana. I was healing after losing my mother to cancer when I was 20. Diana was a well-established specialist grief and loss counsellor, and as we connected over cups of tea, she shared her thoughts and kind words freely with me. Our time together blossomed into a friendship which has become very dear to me.

After living overseas for some years, I returned home to Australia, and Diana offered both her time and mentorship to me as I looked to forge my own next steps. I had the privilege of working alongside Diana and experiencing her astute skill in facilitating grief and loss groups, and as she offered guidance to people looking to find their own pathway to healing.

During these times, I shared my own personal triumphs and struggles with Diana, including the winding and, at times, isolating experience of losing a parent at a young age.

Diana's clear voice on the subject was always one of invaluable support. In no small part, Diana's support has contributed to where I am in my current professional life, as a specialist mental health worker at one of the leading mental health organisations in Adelaide. I often reflect on how my personal healing journey and the support I have received enable me to create space for healing in others.

It was no accident that Diana was able to share her guidance with me at such critical times. With a background in psychology, and a Graduate Diploma in Counselling with a specialisation in grief and loss, Diana has run a successful counselling practice in Adelaide for many years. Diana has conducted countless in-person and online grief support groups, drawing on both her extensive training and her own unique journey of loss, burnout, self-discovery and healing—which is what gives Diana such a unique and clear voice in the current body of works on the subject of grief, loss and healing.

I adore Diana's previous books for their clearly written know-how on difficult to approach subjects.

As with her previous works, *A Practical Guide for Grief & Loss* is written to be accessible to everyone, at any stage on your journey of grief and healing.

Diana's guide is refreshingly approachable, and the clear structure to *A Practical Guide for Grief & Loss* enables the reader to navigate grief as their own journey, exploring modern theories and different expressions of grief. *A Practical Guide for Grief & Loss* considers how to be curious about your experience and authentically explore your emotions, and giving you the tools to place yourself in the present, and to be deeply grounded in your experience. At your own pace, *A Practical Guide for Grief & Loss* invites you to move towards a future that is filled with healing and peace.

The underlying philosophy that lies within the book places the emphasis on self-compassion, and on trust in yourself. With the right tools, peace and purpose are possible. Diana Hutchison's clear voice in the healing space is helpful for anyone experiencing grief, and will be a valuable guide for years to come.

Amy McQuade

Community Mental Health Support Coordinator

INTRODUCTION

When I studied psychology at university in the 1980s, I noticed that the emphasis was on the '*what*', not the '*how*'. While university degrees and courses do give you a great overview of current thinking, which enables a holistic approach to practising psychology in the real world, it is always possible to take a deeper dive into one area. I chose to specialise, and followed the individual counselling route. After many years working in this area, I felt lost, experienced anxiety, and became disconnected from a sense of purpose in my life. These feelings were due to burnout, which led to medication for mental health problems. The result of this was that I was no longer able to continue my job as a psychologist, and needed to totally rebuild my shattered self-worth and self-belief. This rebuilding process took a long time.

Once I had recovered, I decided to go back to counselling, but this time with a new focus. Having experienced the death of both my parents, I chose to specialise in grief and loss. I completed a Graduate Diploma and started running grief and loss support groups.

During the years that I have been running these groups, I have learned so much from the participants that has enriched my professional knowledge and my personal life. I am extremely grateful for group members' willingness to share their stories, both within the group and on a wider stage. Some of those stories can be found in this book. Due to confidentiality, all names have been changed.

When 2020 came along and our lives changed, I decided to extend the support available to those in the grief and loss groups to as many people as possible. To this end, I created a series of online programs, and wrote the first draft of this book. The online programs are on an easy-to-use platform and can be accessed at any time, should you wish to engage in taking yourself through your grief journey at your own pace. See the back pages of this book for information on how you can do this.

This book is an introduction to the grief journey and how you can find your pathway to greater peace. Finding your pathway will be unique to you, although the general process may be similar to the journey that others take.

HOW TO TELL IF THIS BOOK IS FOR YOU

You may have experienced loss through death or

some other major loss. This loss may be recent or may have taken place some years ago. Perhaps you have experienced many losses over time. If you are struggling to manage your daily life or are having specific problems that you feel may be related to the losses you have experienced, *A Practical Guide for Grief and Loss* is for you.

A Practical Guide for Grief and Loss introduces you to concepts, ideas, and theories around grief and loss. You may be familiar with some of them. If not, that's okay. Sometimes it can be beneficial to have an idea of where you might sit in relation to a particular theory. For many people, grief and loss creates a feeling of everything being up in the air, so exploring different theories and getting a bit of structure may enable you to feel more grounded.

This book describes the 'what' in relation to grief and loss—what sort of symptoms, thinking, emotions, and behaviours you may experience. There are also in-depth discussions on more general issues that may arise with grief and loss. This book is not a definitive resource, and you are encouraged to explore other books and resources you feel drawn to. However, it is a good starting place to create a clear overview of the experience of grief and loss.

Terms such as 'the mourning process', 'the grieving process' and 'the grief journey' are often used together, but clarifying the meanings is important. The mourning process is related primarily to the outer expression of grief following a loss, which may vary from culture to culture. The grieving process is related more closely to the inner experience, while the grief journey encompasses both of these, and recognises how grief may or may not change over time.

I will be using the terms 'grieving process' and 'grief journey' throughout this book, because everyone's experience is holistic rather than specific.

WHAT YOU'LL DISCOVER

This book is designed to empower you to discover your own unique journey and pathway through grief. Grief does not necessarily go away, nor do you let go of your loved one or of other major losses you have experienced. Your grief journey assists you in finding the processes, practices, and rituals that allow you to work through your emotions and to let go of the pain and struggle associated with grief and loss. What this means is that, as far as possible, you find a different perspective or a new way of looking at your current reality, so you find more peace and purpose within yourself and your life. Whether or not that feels possible right now, it is achievable.

You can give yourself permission to find the ways of healing that work for you. Until you try something, you will never know what the results, consequences or outcomes may be.

My desired outcome from you reading this book is that you gain an understanding that it is possible for you to find your own pathway to healing. Working out what this pathway may look like for you might take some time and self-reflection.

Since you know yourself best, and are your own change agent, it is in your hands to find what will work for you. Keeping an open mind and experimenting with different perceptions, behaviours, and ideas may be the best way to go. Whatever steps you take, always be aware that you need to be kind to yourself, and only engage in new things when you feel ready to do so.

Because grief and your grief journey experience is personal to you, you may find some content is of greater relevance to you, while other content may feel less relevant. If a certain aspect of grief is discussed in more detail than you feel resonates with you right now, then feel free to skip those bits. If your loss is very recent, then you may find that reading the summaries first may help. When you feel ready, you can go back to the beginning and read more thoroughly.

So, let's begin.

CHAPTER 1
YOUR GRIEF JOURNEY

GRIEF MAY BE DIFFERENT THAN YOU MIGHT THINK OR EXPECT

General community perceptions about grieving seem to be that if you lose a loved one or experience a major loss, then you must 'get over it' within a short period of time, which may be around the three-month mark. This perception is not helpful.

GRIEF AFFECTS EVERY AREA OF YOUR LIFE

The idea that you should just 'get over it' is unhelpful because it does not relate to the experience of losing a loved one through death—or, in fact, through the experience of any major loss. This can be particularly true when you lose a long-term partner or a child, because the relationship bond may be especially strong. To some degree the time and length of the relationship can be implicated, but it does not *need* to be. This is because grief and the grieving process is all about the emotion, the relationship itself, and the meanings we place on the loss of that relationship.

How we grieve and take ourselves through our grief journey also depends on our identity, personality, and whether we are willing to give ourselves the opportunity to go through the process of learning about ourselves. This can mean that if we have a general way of managing change and transitions that works, and if we are open to change, there may be a greater ability to start the process sooner rather than later. However, this is only a 'maybe'. Many things, such as expectations and circumstances, as well as our own experiences and the ways in which we interpret our world, will affect all the aspects of how we manage to cope and think about our new reality.

Some key points to note about grief and loss:

- Everyone grieves in their own unique way. Some people may be more expressive, some less so. There is no 'right' or 'wrong' way to grieve.

  You can go through your grieving process in your own time and at your own pace.

- The aim is not to move on from grief. The aim is to move *through* it. You don't suddenly stop loving your loved one—or anything else you have lost. As David Kessler says, 'Love never dies'[1]. You will not forget.

However, processing your grief does mean letting go and releasing the negative emotions that are causing you the intense pain that arises. It is possible to separate the object of your attachment from the pain and suffering that arises from the loss of your attachment.

- Grief—or rather, the grieving process—takes time. The more consciously you do it, the better. It is not suddenly over and done in a short time frame.

Sometimes it takes many months or even years before you feel as though you are managing your life better. The grief does not disappear, because your love continues. What may be more likely to disappear through processing your loss is all the other pain and emotions that are not specifically related to the person themselves. This is because there are so many aspects and factors that impinge on the whole time around the death and the memory of the person you have lost that need to be sorted through and processed over time. Again, it is a very individual thing. As we will see, some of these factors are related to the relationship itself, as well as relationships with other people around you—whether family or otherwise—and the circumstances and situations involved.

- It is best to reach a state of willingness to accept the reality of your current situation. This is what is involved in processing grief. It is often a difficult task. Sometimes it is difficult to accept the loss, and coming to terms with what is happening can be confronting and challenging.
- Social support is extremely important, to create opportunities for you to feel heard, listened to, and understood. Quality over quantity is advisable.

  Ask for support from professionals if you need to. Grief and loss are not things we can always manage on our own. You don't need to expect yourself to do so.
- Some people may become stuck in their grief and unable to manage their lives. This can be because they do not realise they are able to ask for extra support. Perhaps they believe that everyone does the same thing in grieving, and there is no way of getting better. However, there is a way of getting better, and this is achieved through *reaching out and asking for support.*

These points will be explored further throughout the book.

WHAT IS GRIEF?

Grief is the emotion we feel when we lose someone or something dear to us. It is a natural process we all go through. However, unless you allow yourself to go through the mourning process, there are occasions when that well of grief will spring up and take you by surprise, sometimes when you least expect it.

Grief requires processing and making sense of. This is because our brains have a particular patterning that includes those relationships we have in our lives. When the pattern is changed—as it is when someone or something significant is no longer present in our life—this causes disruption.[2] This, essentially, is the grieving process: the making sense of the change that has taken place and the rewiring of our brains so that the pattern is adjusted, allowing us to manage daily life in a more adaptive way.

Grief is not unique to humans. All creatures appear to be affected by it. It relates to the physical loss of a very strong emotional bond—a bond we call love. We know that our pets mourn, as do other animals, from elephants to primates to birds. Just because we are the only animals able to voice our grief, this does not mean we are the only ones who feel it.

WHAT IS THE MOURNING PROCESS?

The mourning process is the time that you are obviously and outwardly grieving your loss. It is important to draw the distinction between grief, the feeling, and the mourning process itself, which is what you are going through when you experience loss—and particularly a major loss. It may be helpful to think of the mourning process as the time when you are in some way consciously processing your loss but in an outward manner. This is because the mourning process may not always happen immediately after a loss, and in fact may occur a little while or even a long time later. Since our society usually expects people experiencing major loss to recover quite fast, I'll refer more to the grieving process, which relates to your inner experience. This is essentially what matters most.

Grief and the grieving process are two separate things. The grieving process is the period of reconciliation that you go through to find acceptance of your situation and your new reality[3].

I will be using the phrases 'grief and loss journey' and 'grief journey' throughout the book. The phrases reference the process of grieving—not the grief itself. The grief itself may not actually change, but the processing and making sense of your loss (which forms a new pattern in your brain in relation to your loss) will enable you to feel more like yourself and to manage life so that you feel empowered and in charge of your own healing. This means that how you experience yourself and your life is likely to be much better once you have completed this process, in comparison to your experience of yourself and your life at the beginning of the process.

YOUR GRIEF JOURNEY

If you have not previously experienced the kind of loss you are currently experiencing, it is likely to be unknown territory. If you have experienced a similar kind of loss, then you may be able to call on inner resources if you know what may work for you. In any case, even if you have experienced a similar loss, it doesn't mean that the grief you feel for this loss will be lessened. Every loss is different, because every relationship is different—sometimes drastically different from any other relationship in our lives. In addition, our relationships with our loved ones and our relationship with ourselves evolve over time, so our relationship with every single person in our lives is likely to be multi-layered.

The important thing to note is that whatever you are experiencing right now, however you are feeling, and however you are managing, is absolutely fine. You are not broken, and if it seems as though you are, remind yourself that you are going through a really difficult time. When you are grieving, what is most beneficial is to treat yourself with kindness and compassion—as you would treat a good friend.

You know yourself best, and if you contemplate your needs for a few moments in stillness, without rushing, then you may be able to come up with some ways of taking care of yourself that could be good for you right now. Sometimes, just sitting with your feelings for a while and acknowledging them can be enough, whether or not you share these feelings with others.

DEATH OF A LOVED ONE

A Practical Guide for Grief and Loss places a focus on any kind of major loss. This includes loss through death. Many aspects of grieving any loss are universal. Although there are some distinct differences between the experience of the death of a loved one and the experience of other major losses, *A Practical Guide for Grief and Loss* addresses as many factors as possible that are relevant to all. Where such factors are specific to particular losses this will be mentioned. To ensure the book is relevant to you and your experience of grief and loss, you may consider the examples given, make a comparison to your own situation, and see what applies to you and what does not.

THE FINALITY OF DEATH

A person close to you dying means the loss of human life. It means the loss of a relationship that may have spanned years or decades. And it may involve the loss of a family member or a dear friend.

There is also a finality to someone's death, because even though we know that *everyone* dies eventually, we can never have the same relationship with that person ever again. Usually, there is a strong attachment involved when the grief is very intense. This attachment doesn't have to be entirely positive. Grief still comes in if there has been a complicated and difficult relationship. In fact, even if there is very negative emotion attached to the relationship, such as hate, grieving may still be required in making sense of the past or current reality.

RELATIONSHIP FACTORS

The strength, length, and quality of the relationship are important aspects to consider. Again, your own unique way of grieving will also depend on how you manage your grief, the coping strategies you are able to call upon, and the social support you have.

Since each person has their own family members, friends, associates, work mates, and colleagues, as well as their own beliefs and experiences, each of us will interpret the world in our own unique way. This is especially true when it comes to a death.

It is the case that we cannot change what has happened in our past, but we can change our *perceptions* about what happened. When someone dies, the circumstances around the death, what happened leading up to the death, and what happened after the death—right up until this present moment —all need to be processed as part of your grief journey. *This is your grief story.*

MAJOR LOSSES NOT THROUGH DEATH

When it comes to grief and loss through experiences other than the death, the loss may be something we identify with, such as employment or career, a home, possessions, or health. There are many others, too. We may see any of these losses as a threat to our survival, whether physically, emotionally, mentally, or psychologically. This threat may well be traumatic. However, when death is *not* involved, then there may be a greater *apparent* possibility of renewal, to some extent. This is because—generally speaking—the death of someone close has a final element and it seems that other losses may be easier to bounce back from, although this is not always the case.

For instance, losing employment also creates the possibility of finding other employment, however difficult this may be. Retiring from a loved career provides the opportunity to live a different life. Breaking up with a partner brings possibilities of finding another person to share your life with, or to take on different opportunities.

HOW LOSS CAN BE TRANSFORMATIVE

Any grief experience may be a catalyst for you to free yourself from whatever has been holding you back in life generally. This may be because when you start to explore your life and yourself more, your perspective may expand and you may start seeing things in a new way. This means that you can be more open to what is around you and thus likely to discover more opportunities and more ways of seeing yourself in a new light.

All losses or transitions in life can provide us with opportunities to recreate ourselves and to become more self-aware. It is essentially an invitation for healing yourself on all levels or transforming yourself in some way. Whether you pay attention to this opportunity or not is totally your choice, and may depend on your situation and loss.

Of course, with some forms of loss, the circumstances may be that the process will simply require you to grieve for what you no longer have. This would be the case if you become estranged from family members, had a family member or friend go missing, or if you had an accident or health crisis where you lost physical or cognitive function. Even in these situations there are opportunities to re-evaluate your life, and what it is you want from it now and into the future. There is always the possibility of doing your best and being your best no matter what.

THE COMPLEXITY OF LOSS

It is the case that any kind of major loss can be very complex, with the potential for trauma and other aspects, some of which may include the possibility of renewal to varying degrees. However, it is the case that the process of grieving the death of a loved one or someone close can be more easily clarified than some other losses. It is also highly stressful because, to some degree, society is averse to talking about death. It seems to be a taboo subject, at least in the modern Western world. This may be one of the reasons why people, and especially those who have not yet experienced a major loss or the death of a loved one, often don't know what to say to those who do experience such a loss. Where this is the case, conversations can become awkward.

EMBRACING THE CALL OF GRIEF TO SELF-TRANSFORMATION

While death can bring trauma with it, or exacerbate

existing trauma, the grieving process may become complicated through a number of different factors.

All losses *you* experience as major are exactly that. Since everyone grieves in their own way in all circumstances, it is really *your experience* that matters, not how other people—whoever they may be—view your loss.

Essentially, what this means is that making comparisons between your loss and someone else's does not make a great deal of sense. It's unfair to say to someone that your loss is bigger than their loss, like some kind of one-up-man-ship. And equally unfair to minimise or diminish your experience by framing your loss as insignificant in comparison to someone else's. For you to say to yourself that other people have it worse is disregarding your own pain. You need to acknowledge to yourself if your loss is intensely painful, *then that it what it is.* Each person's loss is exactly how they experience it at whatever point they are in their life. Not discounting anyone's pain—including your own—is best. This means that dealing with what is real to you is the key to processing the pain of loss in a way that leads to healing.

CERTAINTY VERSUS UNCERTAINTY

Although life is inherently uncertain, we still like

to enjoy some idea of predictability in our lives. Certainly, this is what our brains are geared to do—to allow us to predict what is going to happen and get us prepared for what is coming up very soon (this can be the next few seconds, minutes or whenever). Predicting what is going to happen can mean the difference between life and death. On a less dramatic scale, predicting what might happen could mean the difference between feeling ok about yourself and feeling embarrassed in a social situation, for instance. Whatever we are doing through the day, we make predictions that feed into our expectations and are, in turn, influenced in the complex network that is our brain.

As humans, we like stability in our lives. Perhaps some people like this more than others—but generally speaking, if we feel safe and can predict what is going to happen tomorrow, then we will not feel as much stress. When everyday life becomes uncertain, and when we don't feel as though we have enough resources to survive, then the uncertainty creates anxiety, fear, and stress. One recent instance of this was the COVID19 pandemic, which resulted in mental health problems skyrocketing[4].

Whether this uncertainty is embedded in one experience of grief and loss or on a wider scale, the uncertainty in any situation is problematic for your mental wellbeing. This is because when there is uncertainty—equating with anxiety and fear—the adrenals are releasing stress hormones such as cortisol that put you into 'fight or flight' mode. When you experience chronic stress, such as when you experience loss and are going through a complex mourning process, then there is a greater likelihood of being affected by this on a number of levels. This will be explored later in the book.

HOW WE FORM ATTACHMENTS TO OTHERS

We are social beings and thrive in relationships with one another. We are wired to pay attention to other people, to form relationships, and to bond. We invest in relationships, care deeply, and love others. We also have attachments to whatever we have in our lives that makes us feel secure, safe, and happy.

Family, friendships, community, society, and sense of belonging all play a part in our attachments. Therefore, these may all impact how we feel when disruption occurs through loss. As we go through life, we may experience major transitions that others experience. For example, an empty nest, retirement, and relationship break-ups, as well as losses through death and social disruptions—whether man-made or natural disasters. These can all disrupt our attachments and sense of belonging.

ATTACHMENT THEORY

Attachment theory started out with John Bowlby[5], and has been researched and worked on over time. It is now recognised worldwide as the central theory that explains how infants' early relationships with their parental figures imprints and affects all future relationships. It is the case that how we may respond to loss, whether the loss of a loved one or any other loss, is dependent upon our early attachment histories. We incorporate patterns of thought, emotion, and behaviour that we learnt back then into our being. What this means is that we may have different attachment styles that may lead to either healthy or not so healthy relationships. How we were perceived by caregivers also affects how we perceive ourselves. These aspects all affect how we relate to others.

In brief, there are four attachment styles. These attachment styles describe specific approaches to relationships, which tend to be stable over time and provide us with a template for developing and maintaining important relationships[6].

1. **Autonomous Attachment**: Here, as an adult, you are able to maintain a balance between self-reliance and relying on your important others. This means that you may choose to manage a situation alone or with others. Additionally,

there is a sense of autonomy and an ability to keep up relationships continuously, whatever they are.

2. **Dismissive Attachment**: With this style, you place more focus on protecting your independence and personal control, and may diminish the importance of relationships. Thoughts are more centred on your own personal achievements and interests. Emotions are seen to be less important, while reasoning and logic are more important in managing life.

3. **Preoccupied Attachment**: You tend to focus on the relationship to the exclusion of your independence. As your sense of autonomy isn't well developed, you may be insecure and unhappy in these relationships. There can be a focus on past relationships, without an ability to lessen the influence of them in your present relationship. Emotions are seen to be more important than reasoning and thinking.

4. **Unresolved Attachment**: An unresolved attachment occurs when an event happens in a current relationship that reminds you of a previous, similarly stressful event in a past relationship. That is, it is an unresolved pattern that may come from any of the above three styles. What this means is that there is a

disrupting effect on the way you function in your current relationship. This can then set up a series of exchanges that create similar themes or patterns in relationships over time.

When we become aware of these unresolved attachments, there is always the opportunity to seek ways and processes to change past behaviours to find a more secure and autonomous style of functioning in relationships. There is always the possibility of healing the past and changing perceptions, expectations, and emotions within to become more authentic and to move to a more secure relationship with yourself.

Your relationship with yourself is truly a primary factor in how you relate to the world.

Of course, there are other factors that have influence on us as we grow, including cultural, societal, gender roles, and many others. These all add to the multi-layered humans that we are.

ATTACHMENT THEORY RELATED TO GRIEF AND LOSS

As adults, the way we are affected by grief may be affected by our attachment style and the closeness of the relationship, among other factors. It could be an interesting exercise to consider your relationship to your loved one or the general patterns of your relationships to people and things, and see if you discover themes relating to the above attachment styles.

If you are interested in this area and want to investigate it further, please see the noted references for this chapter, located at the back of this book.

FINAL THOUGHTS

Grief is a natural emotion and something we all experience. However, each person grieves in their own unique way. There is no right or wrong way to do it. There are a number of factors that influence the intensity of your grief, and the way you go through your grief journey. These factors include your attachment style, the circumstances around your loss, the closeness of the relationship to your loved one, and how strongly you identify with whoever or whatever you have lost.

Keep these ideas in mind and let them percolate. In the next chapter, we will explore a variety of theories on grief and loss.

CHAPTER 1 SUMMARY

- Everyone grieves in their own way. Some people may be more expressive, some less so. There is no right or wrong way to grieve.

- The aim is not to move on from grief. Love does not die. You will not forget. However, by releasing the negative emotions that are causing you pain, you move through the grieving process.

- The grieving process takes time. The more consciously you do it, the better.

- You will find progress if you can get to a state of being willing to accept the reality of your current situation.

- Social support is extremely important, as it creates opportunities for you to feel heard, understood, and listened to. Quality over quantity. Ask for support from professionals if you need to. You can't always do it on your own, and you shouldn't expect this of yourself.

CHAPTER 2

THEORIES ON GRIEF AND LOSS

*People don't need to fit into a theory.
Theories need to fit around people.*

A theory can provide a structure and open up ways of thinking about the truth of a situation. When it comes to the human experience, because we are complex and many aspects may be impacting a situation at the same time, theories may or may not be personally beneficial. It could be expected that a good theory would be able to explain—and perhaps predict—what it is that most people experience, and therefore may help to provide strategies and methods for treatment or healing.

With scientific experiments, there is usually one model that becomes a generally accepted model, which is tested many times. When these experiments show consistent outcomes and results this indicates the theory's validity for use in that particular field.

It may take time for some theories to be accepted by the majority of the scientific community. However, the more a theory is tested and continues to show validity, the more likely it is to be accepted.

Even in science there is a gradual movement forward in what is generally accepted as 'reality'— or the way that everything works as predicted in a particular theory and situation. This is the reason why there is increasing knowledge of our world. Scientists continue to explore and elaborate on different theories and situations because they know that there is no end point to what can be discovered.

When there are anomalies and situations that are not captured in a particular model, other theories may be useful in describing and explaining what the results show and mean. When new theories show better explanations and provide greater understanding, these theories may be adopted as a new, updated model.

Theories are essentially working models of what we perceive as our reality, in relation to a particular field of endeavour.

When the subject relates to the physical world, it is often a fact that theories are on more 'solid ground' than theories in the social and psychological fields. Even so, recent research in these latter areas has been improving, particularly in the area of neuroscience. Human beings are complex, and many different variables need to be accounted for to give a reliable and valid result in this field of human experience and behaviour. The more specific and focused the experiment, the more likely it is that a reliable and valid result from testing that theory may eventuate. However, what this means is that consistent results over many studies are required.

THEORIES ON GRIEF AND LOSS

General theories on grief and loss have followed people's experiences over time, and seek to encompass numerous possibilities. Some theorists have been clinicians first, while others have worked exclusively on the research side. There are a number of theories that can be useful in explaining what happens for people when they experience a loss.

The important point to note is that although grief counselling or grief therapy may be informed by theory, this doesn't mean the person needs to conform to the theory. The theories need to fit the person and their experience. It is also worth mentioning that most theories on grief and loss concentrate on the death of a loved one. A few theories accommodate other losses too.

With the following theories, it may be of interest to see which ones make the most sense to you. If one or two resonate, then take these and see how your experience fits with what you know about your grief journey. The ones that feel most closely aligned with your experiences may give you some sense of where you are currently, and what may be coming up next.

Most of the theories in this area of loss may be classified as stages, phases, tasks or processes.

With stage theories, you may find yourself going through the first stage, then the second, and so on.

Phase theories are similar to stage theories, but the way in which you move between phases tends to be a bit more flexible and may not be as linear.

Task theories are even more flexible and can be independent of one another, so you may not need to do one task before the next.

Process theories are more of a dance between the processing of grief and loss on one hand, and managing other aspects of life on the other.

ELISABETH KÜBLER-ROSS

Elisabeth Kübler-Ross first explored the now-famous **Five Stages of Dying**.

While her original investigation concerned people who were in the process of dying, these stages may also be thought about in terms of what the survivors experience as well. After her book, *On Death and Dying,*[7] she and David Kessler applied these stages to survivors[8]—meaning those who experienced the death of someone close. From this, they created the five-stage theory, involving the stages of: denial, anger, bargaining, depression, and acceptance. The idea is that people go through the stages in order. The stage of grief that someone is experiencing may be clear to an observer, or to the person themselves.

For some people it might be difficult to recognise which stage comes first and what is going to come next. The first stage, denial, may be easy to identify for most people, as it is usually the initial reaction we have to learning of a death. Whether all other stages are experienced in order is arguable. In recent times, David Kessler[9] has suggested that the stages were never meant to be fixed, but are a looser arrangement that people may drop in and out of.

Elisabeth Kübler-Ross and David Kessler: Five-Stage Theory of Grief:

1. **Denial**
2. **Anger**
3. **Bargaining**

4. **Depression**
5. **Acceptance**

David Kessler has since added a sixth stage[10]. This sixth stage is 'meaning'. In this stage, meaning is explored and worked out. This exploration of meaning certainly makes sense, and could be seen as improving and elevating the theory. With the addition of the sixth stage, the theory now comprises:

1. **Denial**
2. **Anger**
3. **Bargaining**
4. **Depression**
5. **Acceptance**
6. **Meaning**

Going through the stages:

1. The theory suggests that when you experience the death of a loved one, you first go into denial. You might feel that it's not true, that it's impossible, or otherwise negate the reality of the loss.
2. The next stage is anger. The feeling in this stage may be 'Why?' Anger can be directed towards the person who has died, those involved in the circumstances leading to the death, God, or oneself.

3. In the bargaining stage, the person makes a promise or deal with themselves, with God, or with some other force, hoping for the loved one to return. The bargain may involve being good or doing something to negate the reality in any way possible. The thinking here is, 'If I'd only done XYZ, then it wouldn't have happened. So, if I now do ABC, can my loved one return?' Another thing that may happen is thinking you see your loved one, perhaps on a crowded street, but then you realise it can't be them.
4. In the fourth stage, depression, reality is sinking in more, and feelings of sadness, helplessness, and hopelessness may come in.
5. In the acceptance stage, the person decides there is nothing to be done and they have no control over what is happening. This means that coming to terms with the reality of the situation is necessary.
6. With the sixth stage, meaning, more understanding is gained about the life of the loved one, the significance of the loss to the mourner, and how this can all translate to create a different way of moving forward in life for the person who has experienced the loss.

JOHN BOWLBY

Another theory posited by John Bowlby[11] is based on attachment theory, as Bowlby was particularly interested in growth and attachment from birth onwards.

Bowlby suggests there are four phases of grief. These are:

1. **Emotional numbing and initial disbelief**

   An initial period of numbness and disbelief serves to delay the onset of extreme emotional pain incurred by the loss.

2. **Yearning and searching**

   As the numbness dissipates the mourner becomes consumed with thoughts of the deceased.

3. **Feelings of disorganisation and despair**

   Attachment behaviours that were implicated in the relationship between the bereaved person and the deceased are realised to be redundant.

4. **Reorganisation**

   In order to reach this stage, one must have fully realised and accepted the loss. Slow and steady change begins to take place as the mourner actively pursues their own life interests. Hope is seen and realised.

In this theory, each person manages their loss in accordance to their relationship with the loved one, in context of their attachment (and their attachment style). With phases, there is once again the implication of an order in which things are experienced—perhaps in a passive way, rather than in an active and experiential manner. These phases are not necessarily fixed, but have some sort of order to them, so that the first phase occurs first, followed by the others more or less in order, although the endings and beginnings of the next phase may be blurred and may overlap. These phases are shifts in emotion and thought processes, which may be quite common.

J. WILLIAM WORDEN

Worden[12] is another practitioner and researcher, and presents his own theory which involves four tasks that people experiencing loss need to navigate.

Worden suggests that these tasks don't necessarily need to be done in any order, although the first one is a good starting point—at least in the capacity of appreciating the reality of the loss on a mental level. The tasks may be explored and processed in any order, on multiple fronts, and may be revisited multiple times.

WORDEN'S FOUR TASKS OF GRIEF ARE:

1. **Accepting the reality of the loss**

    We need to accept that reunion with the deceased

is impossible. Acceptance has to be on two levels: mentally and emotionally.

2. **Processing the pain of grief**

   Working through the pain of grief means facing the intense emotions that arise from accepting the reality of the loss. Many different emotions can occur, including anger, anxiety, guilt and loneliness.

3. **Adjusting to a world in which the deceased is missing**

   Mourners may not be aware of the many different functions the deceased had in their lives. These roles reveal themselves gradually.

4. **Finding an enduring connection with the deceased in the midst of embracing a new life**

   The mourner's relationship with the deceased needs to be moved from the present to the past, so that memories form the link to the deceased. What this means is that rather than having an external relationship with the person, it now becomes an internal one.

   Emotionally relocating the deceased to the past gives the mourner the chance to refocus some attention on other areas of their life, and to establish new emotional connections.

GOING THROUGH THESE TASKS

In processing these tasks, in the initial sessions of my grief and loss support groups, some members have been able to *accept the reality of their loss* on a mental level. However, in the early stages of the grieving process they often have great difficulty accepting the loss on an emotional level. There is always a great difference between understanding a concept in our minds and understanding this same concept in our hearts. It is for this reason that a lot of processing needs to take place before it is possible to move from one understanding to the other.

Processing the pain of grief can be difficult. It may require setting time aside, seeking professional support, finding social support, and providing self-care. Many different things may come up as you grieve, and many symptoms may emerge that relate to your grief process. These will be explored in the next chapter.

Worden's third task, *adjusting to a world in which the deceased is missing,* reveals many aspects as time goes on. In the initial stages, some of my group participants have found that losing their partner means there can be feelings of extreme overwhelm when having to negotiate things like home repairs, car maintenance, cooking, or budgeting, since their partner used to take responsibility for these tasks.

Over time, they become more self-reliant as they find they can manage these tasks themselves, or—in the instances where they cannot develop the skills—as they become more confident in seeking assistance from professionals.

Navigating the fourth task, *finding an enduring connection with the deceased while finding a new life,* is another task that is repeatedly addressed. It does take time to sort through how to create a new identity, and to work out what you really want to do and what you realistically are *able* to do.

This process takes curiosity and exploration. Firstly, the process involves finding a sense of how you can move from the previous reality of having a physical connection with the person to creating an inner connection with them, so that the relationship moves from an external relationship to an internal one. This may be more difficult for some people than others. However, through processing emotions and becoming more accepting of the new reality, it does become easier to contemplate how you can do this best. It may be that in the honouring of your person's memory or life, something arises that holds meaning for you, which makes it more possible to make the shift from an external to an internal relationship.

In the second part of this task, finding a way forward to having more purpose or peacefulness in your life might include exploring all your past dreams that may have remained unfulfilled. Sorting out whether you are still interested in these now, and exploring those that you *are* interested in with more focus, can give you a sense of what your future could look like. This is by no means a passive time, but one of exploration and taking action, even if the action you take is not drastic. It may look like reading different books, exploring a variety of unfamiliar topics and subjects, finding new social connections or even learning and developing new skills.

In this process of exploration, you can find and discover a new sense of self through transforming parts of yourself and your identity. This can be achieved through moving outside your comfort zone.

This is how growth occurs through any major transition. Loss is one transition that we all experience at some time in our lives.

DUAL PROCESS THEORY

A more recent theory is the Dual Process Theory[13]. This is not so much a stage, phase or task theory, but a process. It suggests that the way bereaved people experience grief is really an oscillation between paying attention to their grief and paying attention to their life. Thus, the style of grieving is fluid.

Since everyone grieves in their own way, with some people being more expressive than others, the Dual Process Theory sees grief as a very individual thing. Those people who may be less expressive can be seen as more instrumental (or cognitive) in their mourning process and style, while those who are more expressive can be seen as more emotional. In general, it may be the case that males may be more instrumental and females more expressive. However, everyone contains both of these styles and oscillates between them during the mourning period. No one way is better than the other. Both are required and useful in the managing of our emotions, life, and situations.

This theory opens up the idea that whatever and however you grieve is absolutely fine, and that if you feel stuck in one way of processing your emotions, you can try something different.

What this means is that when feeling particularly stuck in pain, it could be beneficial to do something practical about self-care or to focus on something that will make a difference to your daily life. Thus, engaging more in the life side, rather than remaining in the pain of grief. The other way can also sometimes be a good idea. When you are totally focused on attending to daily living and not processing your pain, changing your focus back to your grief processing could be warranted. This would allow you to make some more progress in your grief processing, and would mean you are not avoiding it.

You don't have to wallow in your pain. You can use distractions, such as work, hobbies, sports, socialising or anything else that you feel you can manage at this time. To be distracted for a while can be useful, so you can understand that your life is continuing and that this also needs attention and focus.

OTHER SIGNIFICANT LOSSES

If you've experienced other kinds of loss rather than a death, it could be likely that the best theories to think about for your loss would be a combination of a bit of Bowlby, but perhaps more of Worden's Task Theory. In the event of any kind of loss, in the latter theory, the first task would be accepting the reality of the loss. If, for instance, you have lost a job through being fired or retrenched, then particularly if this is your dream job or dream career, the initial experience is likely to be shock and numbness, and having difficulties in understanding how and why this has happened.

This would mean that the first task would be to accept the reality of the loss—and not just on the mental level, but also on the emotional level. Once this has been achieved (at least on the mental level), then it would be time to experience the pain of the loss, and what it means for you to have had this occur at this point in your life. There can be intense periods of anxiety and fear in relation to what the results will be for you, given your circumstances, financial situation or living situation. Despair and despondency can come in here, too. This is all working through the pain of grief.

As you can see, this pattern may also fit reasonably well with Bowlby's theory, but with the focus on utilising the stages in relation to a significant loss other than the death of a loved one.

Worden's third task, of adjusting to a world in which what is lost is missing would, in this example of the loss of employment, include exploring other avenues, looking and searching for more information, finding retraining options, thinking about what skills you have that could be transferable, and coming to terms with the differences between what you previously had and what you have right now. Then the fourth task would be finding an enduring connection between your identity then and now, while embracing new situations and a new version of yourself.

LAST THOUGHTS

As previously mentioned, theories may be useful in a practical sense where you can make sense of your own experience and add meaning to it in your understanding of where you are, before gaining perspective on what might be coming next along your grief processing pathway.

Making sense of your experience on a day-to-day level can give a practical way of thinking about how and what you are currently going through. This means that finding a clearer picture of what your experience feels like can allow you to reduce the stress and worry that may arise when you are unsure or uncertain of what to expect.

In the next chapter we will look at different ways grief may be expressed, including some symptoms that you may or may not experience yourself. Because everyone is different, you may find different symptoms affect you more or less intensely than other people you know.

CHAPTER 2 SUMMARY

- Exploring theories may be useful in the context of relating to and exploring different perspectives.

- You don't need to fit the theories; the theories need to fit your experience.

- It may be that some parts of a particular theory are more relatable than others.

- You can pick and choose what you want from one theory or from multiple theories in order to make more sense of what you are going through.

- Sometimes theories can give you a sense of what may be coming up on your grief journey.

CHAPTER 3

DIFFERENT WAYS GRIEF SHOWS ITSELF

INTRODUCTION

While everyone grieves in their own way, your experience of grief may be expressed through any level of your being. You may be surprised at how pervasive your symptoms are, and even how intense.

Symptoms may arise on any level—physical, emotional, mental, behavioural, and spiritual. This is because grief affects us on all levels. However, because we may have preferences for how we interact with the world, we may be blind to other kinds of factors that we are not used to experiencing or utilising in our normal daily lives.

GRIEF IS A TOTAL AND HOLISTIC STATE

You may not be aware that what you are experiencing

is a result of your grief. It may take some time to realise that it is related in any way. This is because any major loss that brings change into our lives can lead to us finding ourselves in completely new situations with regard to having particular thoughts, emotions, or physical changes. As a result, these changes can bring in symptoms that may be baffling to us. For instance, you might become ill or experience some other physical symptoms that you don't immediately see as a part of your grief.

- Depending on your personality and usual ways of communicating, grief may hit you harder than you expected. You may not even realise how hard you have been hit. It can be possible that you feel you are coping well emotionally, and then some event may occur which seems to come out of the blue, when in actual fact it happens because you are unconsciously or consciously stressed, or not paying attention to what you are doing as a result of the grief you are experiencing.

- Stress can be particularly problematic when it becomes chronic, but even acute stress can cause your immune system to become suppressed[14]. When this happens, your immune system is not able to protect you as well as usual. In the short term, stress can mean you catch colds or flu more easily than normal. Sometimes, in the longer term or when you have chronic stress, this can lead to worsening health conditions[15]. It is a good idea to make sure self-care is a priority. When you are grieving, you may not feel like prioritising self-care, but this is the **exact time when you should**.

- However, grief and loss cannot only cause issues with health—other bodily systems may also be affected and disrupted. The particular symptoms you find yourself experiencing may be unique to you, or they may be things that others experience too—in a general sense at least.

COMMON SYMPTOMS AND TIME FRAMES

- With grief, what usually happens in the first instance is that you go into shock. This is often followed by numbness. This feeling of numbness is a protective mechanism and is physiological. Numbness is functionally useful because it allows you to carry out the actions you need to take to get through the days following the death or other significant loss. This may include taking action to conform to legal requirements and societal conventions, reallocating day-to-day personal and professional responsibilities, taking on additional responsibilities, arranging funerals, or other things. The numbness may last from the point at which the news or realisation first occurred through the days up to the funeral and perhaps beyond. Again, this will be dependent on your circumstances, the social rituals you are able to engage in, your way of grieving, and the relationship between you and your loved one.

- Many people experience problems with sleep. This is extremely common following a loss.

PHYSICAL SYMPTOMS

- Physical symptoms include but are not limited to: sleeping problems—from excessive sleeping to insomnia to changes in sleep patterns, such as waking early or going to bed earlier than usual. Pre-existing problems with sleep are often exacerbated by grief.

- Another likely symptom is having no energy at all. Feeling physically exhausted also means that you can become more susceptible to illness through your immune system being suppressed due to stress. You may find yourself experiencing headaches, elevated blood pressure, and so on.

Because loss through death involving a close relationship is one of the most stressful life events we experience, it can be the case that our bodies do not cope as well as usual. As a result, we may be more susceptible to illnesses such as colds. Research has shown that stress—and particularly chronic stress—weakens the immune system and decreases our ability to fight disease[16].

- The stress we can experience through major loss is one reason why it's important to be kind to yourself, and to practice as much self-care as possible.

- If you find that physical symptoms arise but your doctor is unable to find anything wrong, it may be a temporary problem that is grief-related. Diet and exercise are among the factors that impact our physical health, so ensure you get enough nutrition and do what you can to keep moving. Eating and exercise patterns may change a lot while you are grieving, and it's good to ensure you keep looking after your body.

BEHAVIOURAL SYMPTOMS

You may find yourself poring over photos of your loved one, setting a place at the table for them, believing you see them on the street, or keeping their room and possessions exactly as they were. These kinds of experiences may happen early on during the grieving process, and are fine. If they are still happening months or years down the track, so that you feel stuck, unable to cope generally, or struggling with a sense of self, then it may be time to ask for professional support.

- As a consequence of being in a state of grieving, it is fairly common to start self-medicating to try and manage the emotional suffering and pain. Examples such as drinking more alcohol, taking prescription medication such as pain killers, and even using illicit drugs may be deleterious in both the short-term and the long-term. Recognising when you are doing these kinds of things and reaching out for support, or finding ways you can reduce the pain using positive coping strategies, can kick-start your healing process.

- Avoiding grief in any way means that it is still there for later retrieval. This is because purposely avoiding thinking about something does not mean that it goes away: it is still in your unconscious and still in your experience. Grief needs sitting with and being with. Grief needs to be witnessed and acknowledged.[17]

- At the start, it can be possible that your grief is all-consuming and your time is spent constantly thinking about your loved one, feeling sad, and yearning for them. However, it is possible to allow yourself to attend to your grief in small packages of time, such as spending half an hour at night looking through photos and mementos or allocating twenty minutes in the morning to let your mind to wander over memories and emotions around your loss.

EMOTIONAL SYMPTOMS

- When grief hits us, many different emotions may arise, including sadness, depression, anger, anxiety, fear, loneliness, hopelessness, abandonment, loss, overwhelm, and rejection. We may be in a space of just not being able to take anything in, and we may feel irritated by or envious of others, because they don't understand our pain or because their problems seem trivial by comparison. All of this is ok. It is important not to berate yourself for these thoughts and emotions. It's just part of your grieving process.

COGNITIVE SYMPTOMS

- After the numbness wears off, the social rituals are completed, and all the activity settles down a bit, that is when another level of grieving kicks in. This is usually by the sixth week. It may be that memories begin to pop into your mind, seemingly of their own volition, and distract you from what you are doing. This is likely to be when you are in the task of *processing the pain of grief*. Memories come in, to be thought about and processed. This particular phase can start a lot earlier or even a lot later. In any case, there is probably more of an intensity of emotion from around the six week to three-month mark that kicks off a new round of experience.

- You may feel that the grief you are experiencing becomes worse.

However, it is generally normal for the intensity of emotion to increase for a while. What this means is that you may be easily distracted from tasks, and it is possible that you forget things or make more mistakes than usual. It can be useful to take this into account. If you are doing a non-essential task, that may be ok. However, if you are not paying attention to something important, such as driving or certain work tasks, it can be an issue.

If you find this is happening, consider what you are able to put in place to prevent any difficulties from arising. Depending on your work and employment situation you may be able to get some more support and a bit more flexibility. It would be a good idea to discuss things with any superiors so that they understand where you are in your grieving process.

On the other hand, if you are able to keep your focus on work or other day-to-day tasks, then having something that holds your focus, keeps your thoughts at bay, and is a distraction for a while, can be beneficial.

- As you go through your day, whatever you are doing, you are likely to find you are triggered by different things that remind you of your loss and your current situation. On one level, this can be distressing. However, on another level, if you take note of the things that trigger you, then you may be able to keep tabs on the ways in which you are healing.

- It is important to note that although you may think you might be going crazy, you are definitely not. Many different kinds of thoughts and emotions can come up very intensely. It is not uncommon for people who have lost someone and who have experienced other kinds of significant loss to have thoughts of not being here, or to have at least mildly suicidal thoughts. This may happen because there is an element of not wanting to feel distressing emotions, and the thinking is that one way to stop the feelings is to not be here. Often, it may be a fleeting thought rather than a serious one. Depending on who—or what—you have lost, and the situation around that loss, this kind of thinking may last for a little while or for a long time. Even if the thought is not something that would be carried out, it can exacerbate stress and create some concern.

SPIRITUAL/SOUL SYMPTOMS

- Regardless of your spiritual beliefs, in times of loss, your beliefs may be shaken or they may be beneficial in how you manage on a daily basis. In either case, this may affect your coping strategies. Beliefs about the world, your faith, and yourself are likely to undergo some re-evaluation during the grieving process. This is absolutely fine. Exploration may be key here, rather than trying to stick to hard and fast rules.

- It is quite common to become a bit spooked

by experiences that appear to be outside your beliefs. If you have lost someone you may have vivid dreams of them, which could open you up to different possibilities of understanding spirituality, faith or religion.

- Some dreams feel extremely real. It may seem that these dreams *are* real, so that you can interpret the experience as a visitation from your loved one's spirit. If this brings you comfort, it as a good thing.

- There are many documented experiences where a partner knows that something has happened at a particular time, and then later finds out that this was the time their loved one died. In life, parents can have intuitions that a child is in trouble, and vice versa, and other close relationships and bonds can be so strong that one person knows when something is happening for the other. These intuitions are not to be discounted.

- Experiences such as these can also occur after the death of a loved one. Whether in dreams or waking life, a loved one who has died can let you know they are okay. Whether you share these experiences or not, keep an open mind and accept that it is possibly a true communication—particularly if it brings you comfort.

After all, there are many things in this world we have not yet discovered, and some things are unknowable.

TIME FRAMES

- There is no real time frame for the grieving process. This is really the phase of mourning your significant loss. Essentially, you don't lose your grief, it stays with you because it is about love and love doesn't just end. The mourning process is the time during which you process the pain of your loss, work through the meanings around it, and discover how you now go forward. A number of people have described the feeling of having a great big hole in their life, but after having gone through the mourning process, other parts of life come into being and other positive experiences are built around the hole so that life feels better[18]. It will always depend on your situation and other factors, such as your general coping strategies, whether you have a tendency to avoid looking at your loss, the circumstances around the death, and where your focus is directed.

- It is always more useful and practical to allow yourself to grieve consciously, and to accept that there are going to be times when you experience sadness, upset, and any other emotions that may come up. However, it is important to note that grief must be witnessed, so sharing your grief story with others who will understand—whether one-to-one, in a support group, or with family members and friends—will enable you to feel heard, listened to, and understood. Reaching out for help when you need it is all about self-care and self-healing.

HOW LONG DOES GRIEF LAST?

- How long is a piece of string? While there is no end time for grief itself, the time frame for the grieving process depends on many factors. These include aspects around the circumstances of the death itself if you have lost a loved one, or the circumstances around the significant loss you have experienced, if it is something other than a death.

- Factors such as suddenness, unexpectedness, trauma, violence, and expectations of self and society, all come into play. For example, the loss of a child can be more difficult than the loss of a parent for some people. Personal aspects also play a part. Your interpretations of the situation around the loss, which may be affected by your beliefs, your emotions, and your attachment style, as well as how much value you place on your roles in the world, will also have an impact, to one degree or another.

ARE YOU YOUR OWN CHANGE AGENT?

- Whether or not you believe you have the ability to take action and effect change in your life will also make a difference. This is essentially what is referred to by psychologists as your *locus of control[19]*. If you have an *internal* locus of control, you will see yourself as being able to be in charge of your own outcomes. That is, you believe you have the ability to take action to effect self-change or to make a difference in taking action so that you can achieve what you want. If you have an *external* locus of control, you will have a tendency to blame others, and see luck as taking more of a part in what happens to you. Having an external locus of control can be problematic, as it is, to some degree, a victim stance. In some situations, others may be to blame or nature may be to blame. There *are* some things that are outside of our control.

However, we all have the ability to take charge of ourselves, to change our perspective on a situation, and to take control in effecting change where possible—essentially, those changes will be in relation to ourselves, in terms of behaviour, thoughts, and emotions. Taking responsibility for yourself is paramount. Make a start on doing this right now.

TRIGGERS

- Over the days, weeks, and months following your loss, you are likely to be triggered by events and situations in your daily life. You might go past a favourite restaurant that you used to frequent, and suddenly find that intense emotions and memories are coming up. If you have lost a partner, you might be triggered by seeing couples together. Songs can also be very triggering. Certain smells, such as a particular aftershave or scent, a TV show you watched together, and many other things, can suddenly remind you of your loss—even if you haven't been thinking of it for the last little while.

- For losses that don't include death, the triggers may be quite different. This is because the kind of loss you have experienced will affect what you are now paying attention to more than in the usual way. To some degree, thoughts are more likely to trigger you than physical reminders. If, for instance, you have lost your job, then thoughts of the secondary losses such as how you will now support yourself or your family may come into your head. This happens because these factors are connected to the meaning you have about what employment gives you. Connections are everywhere.

EFFECTS ON YOUR IDENTITY: HOW YOU VIEW YOURSELF

- With any major loss, and particularly when we feel that we have lost our identity, how we view ourselves and how we relate to the world may drastically change. We almost certainly lose roles. We may also lose beliefs, perceptions, and a sense of purpose. Everything feels upended. As a result, we feel lost in the world.

- It's as though our world has stopped turning, but the rest of the world keeps on going. The sun still rises in the morning, and it's still dark at night. People may tell us that life goes on. But even though this may be true, it seems unfair and unreal—certainly in the phases where we are in shock or feel numb.

- The experience of losing a loved one or the experience of another significant loss may cause you to lose touch with your self-definition, because you are thrust into a new reality with which you are unfamiliar. Relearning your world is important here. This means there is a requirement to develop an understanding of what your world now looks like, to learn how to navigate day-to-day life, and to work as consciously as possible to process your grief in order to redefine yourself in a manner that matches your new reality. However, as it can be very difficult to reframe your world in this way, reaching out for support from others when you need to is crucial.

THE EMBODIMENT OF EXPERIENCE

- While I have outlined some influencing factors that affect how grief may be experienced, this is not the complete picture. As humans, we are not just bits of this and bits of that, we are truly whole and complete. Every part of us is connected to every other part. The mind/body connection is 100%. There is no physical reality as we know it presently without being in a body. We are embodied. You embody yourself.

However, you are more than your body, you are more than your brain, you are more than your feelings, you are more than your thoughts, you are more than your behaviour. Essentially, you are more than the sum of your parts.

- Mind and body are one. They are not separate from each other. Therefore, grief itself may be embodied. It is a part of your experience of reality, and if you pay attention to the whole of your reality, even when you may only be focusing on one aspect (your loss), this could be enlightening.

- Because we have our own experiences, beliefs, values, and ways of interpreting what we perceive in our world, and this being our reality, whatever we forget, repress or want to avoid may be expressed in our bodies. We may, in fact, see our bodies as part of our unconscious. Certainly, memories and experiences may be stored within our body[20]. This relates to the idea of psychosomatic illnesses, and psychodynamic therapy. Our bodies are not all the same in terms of physiology and genes. Each of our bodies is unique in how we react to our environment and our experiences. We may have a particular system, organ, or part of our body that has some level of weakness, and because this part is weaker than the rest of our body this specific part may express the issues we have—whether psychologically or emotionally.

- What this means is that there can be a particular symptom or symptoms you find yourself experiencing that you do not necessarily equate with your grief. Whether you realise or not, shock, emotions, and experiences do affect your body in a physical sense. Many years ago, it was established that the death of a loved one, along with other major losses, are at the very top of the scale of stress-creating experiences[21].

STRESS AND HEALTH

A great deal of research has been done in relation to stress, illness, and health and wellbeing. When we experience stress, so that we are faced with what we perceive as a threat of some kind, the flight or fight response is activated and our adrenal glands release a number of hormones, including cortisol, to prepare us to run if that is what we need to do. Of course, this is all good if we are faced with a life-threatening situation and need to run away, and this probably saved many people in the past when faced with a dangerous animal. However, now we may perceive threats in many other forms. A threat is inherent in the death of someone close, or in other circumstances such as needing to move house, finding alternative means of survival following the loss of a job, or in any other situations that result in us feeling our existence is threatened in some way. This is the case even if it is just how we perceive ourselves and our life.

GOOD STRESS

One thing to know is that we do *need* stress. There is a level of stress that is optimal. Good stress can be seen more as a challenge to rise to in a particular occasion. Perhaps speaking in public, sitting an exam, working and taking action in areas you know and are familiar with. Things like learning new skills, reaching for desired experiences outside your comfort zone, and engaging in life in ways you haven't before are all similar in that you are initiating the action and you are excited to reach more of your potential. These kinds of challenges involve good stress.

CHRONIC STRESS

When you feel out of control and find it difficult to assess what needs to be done in order to negotiate or navigate a situation, particularly when there is also a disruption in your life circumstances and how you see yourself, then what usually happens is you perceive a threat and your body produces stress hormones, which may lead to feelings of anxiety, stress, and fear. Where this occurs over a period of time and becomes more chronic, you may experience more physical symptoms of illness.

RELATING STRESS TO GRIEF AND LOSS

- Immediately after any significant loss, you may experience things like having no energy and having problems eating.

- The disruption of normal circadian rhythms may also occur, so that your sleep is affected. Since the space for quiet occurs when we go to bed or perhaps at certain times of day, having time to think without distractions means that this time can be particularly disrupting. Loss enhances this, and so difficulties getting to sleep may well be experienced as thoughts which come into your mind that feel difficult to manage.

- Disruptions to normal habits and patterns of behaviour may mean that waking in the middle of the night and not being able to get back to sleep could be a problem. This may be accompanied by intense anxiety, sadness, and a feeling of absolute loneliness. These feelings may arise at any time, particularly when you are reminded of your loss

- Additionally, chronic stress can depress your immune system so that you may be more likely to become ill or sick. Things such as catching colds, flu, and other viruses can happen more frequently as a result of a depressed immune system[22].

- It is not just small illnesses that may occur, but more serious ones too. It is the case that a percentage of widows and widowers become seriously ill and die within 6 months or a year of their spouse. To some extent, this can be said to be the remaining partner dying of a broken heart[23].

EXPLORING METAPHYSICAL MEANINGS

- Whether you have an idea about a spiritual world or not, you can add an extra dimension to your thinking on top of what your doctor tells you regarding any physical and psychological symptoms you may experience following a significant loss. This is because everything is connected to everything else: body, mind, spirit, and environment. We live in this world. This world has a context. This doesn't mean there is only one way of looking at something. Many different aspects can be brought into the mix, even if just for contemplation. These aspects can be explored at any time – not just when you are ill or have experienced a loss.

- In a situation where you find you are having some trouble with a specific area of your body, it may be enlightening to consider the metaphysical meaning of this part of the body. Sometimes, when we experience health conditions, our body is being attacked at our weakest area at that time. This does not apply all the time or with all infections and diseases. It may apply if you succumb to something that is unique to you. Additionally, the metaphysical meaning adds a layer of personal interpretation that you can factor into your experience— or not. If it is something that you do wish to consider and explore, there are a number of ways to use spirituality that can give an extra layer of meaning.

PERSONAL EXAMPLES OF ADDING MEANING

Two personal examples of exploring the metaphysical meaning of health conditions that I have experienced include a retinal detachment, which was luckily caught in time and stabilised through laser surgery. When I looked up eye problems in Louise Hay's book, *You Can Heal Your Life*[24], it suggested that there was something I was not seeing. In contemplating this idea, which I did over time, I thought there was probably something in this. When the retinal detachment happened, I wasn't doing any work *on* my business. Just working *in* it. I wasn't seeing how I could move my business forward. After the laser surgery, I started looking at ways to move my business forward. In this way, exploring the metaphysical meaning of the retinal detachment was helpful.

Thinking about different ways of understanding health issues can be of use. It is not, of course, the only thing to consider. It is important to get the right medical treatment, where necessary and when available. Physical causes may also play a large part.

The second event, which occurred some years earlier, happened when I broke my wrist. This was how I found out I had osteoporosis.

When exploring the metaphysical meaning of a broken right wrist, I found that wrist issues relate to movement and ease, and the right side of the body relates to masculine energy. This was something to contemplate, too. I could relate it to boundaries I had with myself and others, so over time I have instigated firmer boundaries with myself and others in my life. In this way, the metaphysical meanings add to self-exploration. It is certainly something you can delve into, if it interests you.

The idea that different illnesses and symptoms having metaphysical meanings behind them was popularised by Louise Hay[25]. Over recent decades, many books have been written about the mind/body connection, how illnesses and diseases occur, and what kinds of healing may be most useful according to the illness. Two of these books include *The Body Keeps the Score*[26], and *Mind Over Matter*[27].

Any metaphysical meaning or spiritual aspect derived from physical symptoms does not ever mean you should not get the proper medical attention and treatment you need.

The psychological and spiritual meanings you derive from physical symptoms may provide the opportunity to expand your healing into different areas of your life, beyond the physical. One reason why psychological counselling helps people heal is that it is possible to work on issues from mind to body *and* from body to mind. We already know it is possible to work from body to mind, because this is what doctors have been doing for a long time. We know that physical treatments such as medicine, diet, and exercise affect the body itself and also affect the mind.

This chapter has explored symptoms that may be experienced by many people, and others which may be unique to you, depending on your physiology, your psychology, and your emotions. A number of factors can be involved in the grief experience which can have an impact on different levels. The importance of self-care and managing stress has also been discussed in this chapter.

In the next chapter we will be exploring the process of grieving, to create a better understanding of how you can move through your own grieving process.

CHAPTER 3 SUMMARY

- Whatever your loss, the intensity of the symptoms that arise for you will depend on many factors.

- Common symptoms you may experience range from: sleep disturbance, dreams, appetite disturbance, and illness; cognitive and thinking problems such as feeling distracted and losing focus; emotional difficulties, such as feelings of anxiety and overwhelming sadness or loneliness; and spiritual difficulties, such as questioning or losing faith.

- You can directly address specific symptoms as you see fit, with help from others where necessary.

- While some symptoms may require intervention, self-care is of paramount importance at this time.

- Taking things one step at a time is a good way of approaching your grief journey.

CHAPTER 4

EXPLORING EMOTION

Can You Identify What Emotion You Are Feeling Right Now?

Throughout our lives, we experience different emotions. We are emotional beings. We cannot make decisions or judgements between two or more choices without an emotional input. For this reason, if you keep on thinking you are wrong to make an 'emotional decision', you can alter this thought. There are, of course, times when we need to use both our head and our heart for decision-making, but there are times when it can be important to go with our intuition[28].

At certain points in our life, when we are bombarded with intense feelings and emotions, it can be difficult to maintain a sense of equilibrium. One such point can be when we experience a major loss or change. When you are struggling to maintain your equilibrium, what are some of the ways in which you can manage your emotions?

WHAT IS AN EMOTION?

The dictionary definition of emotion is 'a conscious mental reaction (such as anger or fear) subjectively experienced as strong feeling usually directed toward a specific object and typically accompanied by physiological and behavioural changes in the body'[29].

Emotions are primary. Emotions influence thinking. The ways in which our thinking is influenced will depend on the situational parameters, including our past experience, the information we have to hand, and our reasoning at the time. These things will help us to interpret the situation and then, if necessary, to take action. Thinking also influences emotion, because your interpretation of the situation will have an impact on the emotions you experience. Negative emotions lead to more pessimistic thinking, especially when the information we have is unclear or unknown. In these circumstances, we may tap into our instinctual negative bias[30].

WHERE DO EMOTIONS COME FROM?

If you are experiencing intense grief right now, skip to the section on Emotions And Loss

Much research in affective neuroscience has been carried out in the last decade, and there is now new thinking about emotions. Although Darwin suggested that emotions are helpful in evolution and natural selection, updated research has found that there are five salient features of emotion that all the animal world exhibits:[31]

1. **Valence:** emotions may be either positive, which means you approach, or negative, which means you withdraw. You can think of the valence feature of emotions as being about pleasant/unpleasant, positive/negative, or good/bad
2. **Persistence:** after the emotion arises, it may continue to be present for some time. For example, this may mean that after you experience a fright, you may continue to be hypervigilant for some time.
3. **Generalisability:** one particular event in which you have a specific emotion may be attached to all such events. For example, if you are bitten by a dog, you may become fearful around all dogs.
4. **Scalability:** an emotion may only be felt a little bit or it may be very big and intense.
5. **Automaticity:** emotions are automatic and come before conscious thought. This means that our body and our unconscious mind interpret situations faster and more accurately than our logical mind.

Our emotional evolution may well have come from what is called the 'core affect'. This term was first coined by psychologist James Russell to describe the sensory state of our being that is a central element of the mind/body connection.

It involves our general feeling of how we are, including sensory and cognitive input from our internal physical environment and our external awareness. We may call it our intuition[32].

Our brains help us to interpret the world around us. Our emotions also guide us to interpret the world around us. Depending on our personal experiences, and all the other factors involved in a situation, we may be right or we may be wrong in our interpretation. Generally speaking, it is more likely that we will misinterpret situations that are *not* life-threatening to us or others, rather than those that are.

On a day-to-day level, one fact we may not realise or be aware of is that the decisions we make in our daily life may be based mostly on our core affect state (that is, how we feel within our environment and what we are currently aware of around us). For instance, it has been shown that if grocery shopping on an empty stomach, you are likely to buy more impulsively—and to buy more snack foods—than when shopping on a full stomach. In this way, our conscious experience is formed by an interaction between our brains and our bodies[33].

Research over the last decade indicates that emotions guide thought. Particularly, Haidt[34] has found primary emotions or feelings that specifically change attitudes in relation to the moral transgressions of others. Primarily, it is the emotion of disgust that drives our attitudes. This demonstrates that emotions are crucial to our ability to live together socially in a peaceful and cooperative manner.

Separate studies have shown that people experiencing more positive emotions such as happiness, joy, gratitude, and awe are more likely to be more generous, take more risks, explore, and be more curious and creative than when feeling less expansive emotions and more negative feelings, such as sadness[35]. When people exercise and interact socially then they are usually happier, too.

When it comes to feeling the more negative emotions, such as sadness or anxiety, we tend to act in accordance with our feelings. This means that although there may be more realistic assessments of some situations, there is a withdrawal of energy going outwards, so that people are less generous, less likely to take risks, and less likely to be curious.

Instead, they are more likely to focus their energy and attention inward[36].

EMOTIONS AND LOSS

When experiencing a major loss, focusing your attention inward is the natural way to work through the tasks of grief, and to process whatever the loss is and the meaning the loss has for you. There is a balance that you need to work out for yourself in relation to how much time you spend looking inward, versus how much time you spend engaging with the world and looking outward. This relates to the **dual process theory** that was explored earlier.

HOW DOES EMOTION RELATE TO PHYSICAL PAIN?

When we experience any kind of intense loss, we may feel emotional pain—and this can express as physical pain. This is because both physical pain and emotional pain light up neurons in our brains in the same area[37]. This means that emotional pain can be felt as physical pain.

Physical pain will become enhanced and be felt more intensely if you focus on it. Research studies exploring aspects of chronic pain sufferers have repeatedly shown that there is an element of emotional pain that appears to make the physical pain more intense[38].

What this means for chronic pain sufferers is that there is an opportunity to take action in order to reduce the experience of your physical pain.

There are a number of ways to reduce the intensity of both physical and emotional pain, which we will explore later.

COMMUNICATING YOUR EMOTIONS TO OTHERS

Naming and labelling the emotion creates more clarity in communication with yourself and others. This is because greater specificity gives greater clarity, and allows you to take the emotion from an internal feeling to an external reality. This means it is understood in an objective reality that you share with others.

When communicating your emotions and feelings, the more accurately you can identify them and name them, the clearer your communication will be and the easier you will be understood. To download a list of emotions to help you on your way with this, go to my website www.dianahutchison.com/shop This download is FREE.

EMOTIONS, GRIEVING, AND THE MOURNING PROCESS

With an experience of a great loss, you may understand why it is difficult not to think about your sad feelings, the loss itself, and the negative emotions that are now coming up for you. Withdrawing from others may be helpful for a short time, but will not be of benefit in the long term. This is because you may not be able to move beyond the thought patterns and emotions of grief by yourself. Have a think about the following and see if you can relate.

EXPERIENCES ARISING FROM THE LOSS OF A LOVED ONE OR FROM OTHER SIGNIFICANT LOSSES.

1. **Holding onto the intense sadness as a way to remember your loved one.**

    Kristina discovered she'd been holding onto her sadness for over ten years, after her father had died overseas. This discovery occurred after she had counselling and was able to grieve 'properly' for him.

2. **Family issues leading to people withholding information.**

    Adelina's parents and siblings lived in a different state. Adelina visited her family, but was not told that her mum had terminal cancer. A few months later, she was distraught when she was given the news that her mum had died, and flew straight home to be with her family. However, she was not allowed to have any input into the funeral, and was very angry about this.

3. Self-medicating with alcohol, drugs, food, or work.

Joanne started drinking heavily when she was caring for her father, who had Alzheimer's. Her drinking increased after his death and escalated even further when her sister was diagnosed with early onset dementia. When she cut back on her drinking, many different emotions came up for her, including fear, anger, sadness, despair, hopelessness, rage, desperation, shame, isolation, overwhelm, self-pity, denial, and shock. However, there were also positive emotions, such as hope, belief, and trust.

4. Thinking about the 'what ifs' and blaming yourself or others.

This is a very common thought process, particularly if you feel that you did or did not do something that could have made a difference. This is essentially the 'searching and yearning' phase of Bowlby's theory. This phase relates to the feelings of guilt you may experience about your actions or inactions leading up to the loss.

After Terry's wife died, he felt very guilty and believed that he should have done more for her when she was still alive.

An important point to note here is that what happened, happened.

Everyone does their best at the time—including you. You could not have changed the outcome at all. If you believe you could have, this is magical thinking. You cannot change the past.

5. Having your eyes opened to a reality you didn't see before.

Leoni was inside the home she shared with her husband, and hadn't realised he had gone outside. When she saw him through the window, she didn't recognise him at all, due to his physical changes following a serious illness. She was totally shocked when she realised that the stranger she was looking at was, in fact, her husband. Her shock quickly turned to horror, devastation, and sadness. She cried—because she felt she had lost the man she'd married.

Leoni eventually came to understand that he was still the man she loved, even though he was more physically fragile as a result of the illness.

6. **Losing a sense of purpose.**

   Bernadette experienced a loss of purpose and identity when she retired. This feeling increased when her husband died. She no longer recognised her value, and felt that all the colour had gone out of her life. As a result, she felt very lonely and anxious.

7. **Feeling lost, angry, vengeful, anxious, guilty, or fearful.**

   Any kind of emotion can arise following a major loss.

   Vijay was forced into redundancy, and was very frightened about what might happen as a result of the unexpected loss of employment. As his partner worked from home, he couldn't find alone-time to deal with his grief.

STRATEGIES FOR MOVING THROUGH HARD TIMES

EMPATHY, COMPASSION, AND KINDNESS

These three emotions are ways of taking action, in relation to yourself and others. If you are not in the habit of being empathic, compassionate or kind to yourself, you may have difficulty extending those same behaviours outwards. If so, it could be helpful to explore these positive emotions and how you can embody them in your life. It may take some time to learn how to be kind, compassionate, and empathic. It is an ongoing process that is not to be rushed. It is to be lived and embodied.

As you are going through life's transitions and struggles, looking after yourself as you would a beloved friend is the best approach. You can choose to heal yourself. Finding the right ways to do this for yourself is what you can now start focusing on.

HOW NEGATIVE EMOTIONS ARE CLEARED DURING THE HEALING PROCESS

In the healing process, many emotions come up around death, loss, and change. These may include guilt, anger, anxiety, and fear, as well as many others. The related thoughts that accompany these emotions may hang around and mess with your head, keeping you in a state of feeling stuck. These emotions and thoughts may be separate from the grief you experience about the loss itself. As a result, it can sometimes be difficult to sort through and let go of these emotions and the accompanying thoughts.

Every emotion is legitimate. Emotions are neither good nor bad, but our judgement labels them this way. All emotions can help us navigate our world, because they can teach us about ourselves and our experiences.

If you don't hold onto emotions, they tend to disappear after a few minutes. Sometimes, if you are aware of an emotion and able to label it, in a few moments it might change, and then you may find you are experiencing another emotion. Often, emotions cycle[39]. This can be somewhat dependant on our core state and our interpretation of our emotions[40].

Following a loss, we need to make sense of our new reality. This includes creating a new pattern in our brain to help us manage our lives now that there is a new situation. This requires freeing ourselves from the loss pattern, and beginning to integrate new perspectives. In order to achieve this, it is important to take some action to help yourself manage life better. Choosing to engage in positive coping strategies is one way to start this process.

STRATEGIES AND TECHNIQUES TO HELP MANAGE STRESS, LOSS, AND LIFE TRANSITIONS

Some of the better coping strategies to move the healing process along are 'Active Emotional Coping Strategies'.

Active emotional coping strategies are the most effective kinds of strategies for managing problems and stressful situations, and include the following[41]:

- **Redefinition:** This is the way of finding something, however small, that is positive or redemptive in a bad situation. This strategy reframes the problems involved to gain a different understanding and perspective.

- **Humour:** When using humour, there is a bit of distance gained through looking at the problem from a new perspective. Rather than being completely in it, you can be a little more outside it.

- **Venting emotions**: Expressing and talking about your emotions can be also very helpful. This occurs in counselling, grief support groups, and other kinds of support groups. In these settings, it may be important to express all kinds of emotions, whether positive or negative. This can help you to gain a more balanced view.

- **The ability to accept support:** This is another effective strategy. It may be one that is difficult for some people. At times, you need to feel it is okay to reach out and ask for help. When the pain of grief is intense or the loss is complex, you should not expect to have to manage these feelings by yourself. *Social support is extremely important.*

- **Meditating and mindfulness practices:** These are very good techniques to help you manage daily life, enabling you to become calmer, more focused, and to increase your health and immune system function.

There are groups around that you might like to join to learn these practices, along with apps such as Calm, and helpful videos and audio guides on platforms such as YouTube and Audible.

ADDITIONAL IDEAS

- **Engaging with the world:** This can be something you don't want to do after a loss. When you feel it is just outside your comfort zone and you are *nearly* ready, this can be the best time to take action.

- **Self-care:** This is another important aspect of finding ways to manage. It is always important, but especially following a loss, because situations may arise where you find yourself not caring so much about yourself. You need to make sure you get enough sleep, eat healthily, and get some exercise. If you are feeling overwhelmed, the best way to manage this is to change your perspective from looking at the forest (the big picture) to focusing on one tree (considering one detail at a time).

- **Journaling:** This is extremely beneficial when working on the process of grieving. It doesn't matter if you just end up with a page of swear words. What you are doing is making your thoughts and emotions more objectified. You are writing them down on a piece of paper, which means you can have an 'observer view' on what you have written. This can, in a sense, make things seem more real. Your thoughts and feelings are not just in your head, but written down on paper. While handwriting is preferable, you could also record your voice on your phone.

The main point of the journaling process is that you are gaining a greater sense of clarity on your own experience and on yourself, and in the process, you are becoming more self-aware.

Utilising all or some of the above strategies, whether you have previously engaged in them or not, will help you to do more processing of your new reality, and to begin to organise and plan how you may wish to manage daily life. This could include doing some journalling for a while, such as writing down your feelings and your thoughts about them, or looking back over the day once it gets to the evening, then making either a written note or a mental note of anything that triggered you, and the emotions and thoughts that came up for you. Even just this process may be of use if you feel that you are wanting to deal with your grief journey by yourself. On the other hand, should you reach out for extra help and support as well, then this journaling and writing will add to the support. Whatever you decide:

THIS MEANS:

- Taking things slowly
- Just one day at a time
- If you can't do one day, then do one hour at a time
- Or one thing at a time (whatever your definition is of one thing)

As much as grief reactions are very individual, so are the strategies and techniques that work best for you. The strategies and techniques need to be applicable to your situation, and it needs to be possible for you to incorporate them into your daily life and routines. They also should suit your temperament. It is about finding the things that work for you. This may mean that you need to try some of these strategies and see which ones you like, and which ones you can continue over time.

COPING STRATEGIES THAT HAVE WORKED FOR OTHERS

Terry found what worked best for him was engaging in relaxation and meditation practices. Over time, realising that he was unable to change the past, he became less hard on himself and the guilt he felt decreased.

Kristina found that blocking it all out and focusing on her studies worked for a time, but after a while, she benefitted greatly from getting information about grief and loss, so that she could see her situation in a new light. Asking for support from professional counsellors was also a big part of her healing.

Adelina didn't feel that anyone could show her a better way to deal with her situation. Therefore, she didn't reach out for professional support. What was special in healing her grief was being given something tangible to remember her mother by.

Joanne found that seeking out support from grief groups and psychologists, paying attention to her own needs, and applying self-care practices started her healing process. Being gentle with herself was also a big turnaround for her. Giving herself time for her creativity to flourish, doing things like yoga, mindfulness, positive self-talk, and spending time in nature were all a part of the process of coming to a kinder and gentler place within herself. Having some keepsakes and honouring her loved ones were also important.

Bernadette found that the most effective strategies were spending time with friends and family, and telephone calls with friends who lived at a greater distance from her. Another strategy that she found useful was sitting alone with her feelings. She tried different strategies that were suggested by professionals and also some strategies she found in the books she read about grief and loss. She also listened to relaxation tapes and music.

Social support came through meeting a new group of friends who had experienced similar losses, feeling safe about talking with them, venting feelings, and sharing stories.

Vijay realised that because one his main difficulties was that he felt he was not making a difference in the world, finding factory work enabled him to change this feeling to some degree. However, due to a sense of loss of identity and feelings of low self-worth, it took time. One of the secondary losses after his redundancy was the strong connections he had made with his former colleagues. Finding distractions was useful. Engaging in study kept his mind active and interested. Structuring his day and finding small jobs to do around the house was also part of the process. Even so, there were still down days for some time.

Eventually, he asked for professional support and saw a psychologist on a number of occasions.

FINAL THOUGHTS

When in emotional pain, it can be important to do a self-assessment in relation to what is going on for you. If you can be a little bit curious about what might work for you in managing the emotions and other things you are finding yourself experiencing, it is likely that you will discover at least one or two strategies which will be useful. When we are in a place of pain or overwhelm, it is sometimes very difficult to get motivated to reach out for professional support or to stop ourselves from self-isolating. However, this is often the time when reaching out for support is most beneficial. You cannot expect yourself to do everything in isolation.

There is the statement that if you keep on doing the same thing, you'll get the same results. Sometimes, action in a different direction is what will create the seeds of change you require to find yourself thinking in a different way, so that you are more likely to see a way out of where you are right now, and find the ways to create more positive management of your daily life.

This chapter has outlined the emotions that may arise following a loss, and general coping strategies that can be useful. In the next chapter we'll explore the grieving process in more detail.

CHAPTER 4 SUMMARY

- Humans are emotional beings and we make judgements based upon these emotions.
- All emotions are valid and legitimate.
- Recognition of particular emotions enhances communication with—and understanding of—others.
- Many emotions come up when we face grief and loss.
- Sometimes, sitting with your emotions allows you to process them.
- What you do with your emotions is what is important, not the feeling of them.
- Strong emotions indicate the importance of self-healing.
- Coping strategies can either improve or hinder the processing of your grief.
- Positive coping strategies include emotionally focused strategies that begin to change your experience of the context of the emotion.
- Emotionally focused strategies include: redefinition, venting emotions, using humour, seeking social support, asking for professional support, meditation/mindfulness, engaging in self-care, and journaling.

CHAPTER 5

THE PROCESS OF GRIEVING

INTRODUCTION

How we grieve and take ourselves through the grieving process depends on multiple factors including: personal factors, situational factors, and the actual loss itself.

PERSONAL FACTORS INCLUDE:

- your personality
- your early conditioning
- your attachment style
- how close the relationship was
- how much empathy you have
- your general emotional sensitivity
- the length of time that has passed since the loss
- the importance of your relationship with—or to—what has been lost

- how closely you identify with whom—or what—has been lost
- the meaning you give the loss
- how you interpret the world around you
- your values and beliefs, including spiritual beliefs and faith
- your usual ways of coping
- your ability to reach out and engage support

SITUATIONAL FACTORS INCLUDE:

- circumstances around the loss
- access to social support
- access to professional support
- whether or not you have dependents
- your access to external resources
- your support system
- whether there are any complicating factors
- the manner of death/loss in relation to social circumstances
- whether you have experienced individual loss or community loss
- social events/environmental disasters
- the manner of death/ type of loss

THE LOSS ITSELF

One way of thinking about this is to consider how much disruption your life has had due to your loss. This relates to your sense of self and the level of stability you have in your life. Where these are totally upended, there are likely to be greater complications as you work to regain equilibrium and a sense of safety.

This is because the greater the effect on us—whether physically or emotionally—the greater the likelihood that we will go into survival mode. The threat is essentially to our sense of self. This alone can be devastating.

Where the situation involves a natural disaster, so that survival needs such as new accommodation, food supplies, and the organisation of finances must come first, it will only be further down the track that the losses involved can be grieved and mourned for.

THERE ARE MANY COMPLEX ISSUES THAT MAY BE INVOLVED

Each person experiencing loss may need to explore their own issues, and although the circumstances around the loss—such as the social context, personal factors and the particular loss—may be straightforward, there are many things that can create more challenging and difficult mourning experiences. These include:

AVOIDING

When we are faced with an issue or problem, such as an experience of loss or a major life transition, then even though this loss may be front of mind for us, there can be a tendency to want to avoid looking at it and or processing it. This can be for a number of reasons.

One of these reasons may be that the pain of the loss is very intense. Whether or not you experience a feeling of being overwhelmed may be governed by factors directly related to your relationship with your loved one, such as how close the relationship was, the strength of the relationship, any conflict within the relationship, and any feelings of ambivalence that existed on one or both sides. Where you have experienced a major loss other than the death of a loved one, these aspects still apply.

This feeling of being overwhelmed may last for a short time or for a long time. It will depend on your beliefs, personality, how you generally cope with life, and what strategies you employ that can be useful or otherwise. Other factors may also be involved, such as your attachment style, the people you have in your life who can support and sustain you, and your way of processing grief.

If you avoid going through the grieving process for any reason, then your grief becomes suppressed and pushed down into your unconscious. It doesn't go away. It waits until you have more space and time to explore and process the grief attached to your loss.

Avoiding and escaping looking at your loss may also occur if you resort to alcohol, drugs, or even become a workaholic in order to block the pain. These are behaviours that repress or suppress grief so that it cannot be explored.

THE NEEDS OF OTHERS

One situation where the grieving process does not always find traction in your mind is when you have commitments to other people, such as when you have a young family or an ageing parent to care for. If you have to consider other people, you may feel that you need to be strong for them. It is absolutely fine for the needs of others to take precedence.

However, at some stage, you will need to give your grief some space and time, so that you can process your pain. You could think about the possibilities of giving yourself some time to do this in small steps, such as setting time aside for this processing every week or every few days. Even half an hour at a time can be of benefit, whether every night, a few times a week or once a week. Every little bit adds up, and in this way, it may be less overwhelming than if you avoid looking at it so that it remains unprocessed and in a raw state, until another loss sparks it off and makes it even more intense.

COMMUNITY CRISES OR PERSONAL CRISES

If you are experiencing the trauma of events that are related to homelessness, natural disasters, war, violence or other kinds of displacement and financial hardship, then any grief processing is necessarily going to come after you have your survival needs met. Maslow's hierarchy of needs[42] puts survival needs right at the bottom of the hierarchy. This means that these needs must be met first before you can even start thinking about anything else. Once there is a bit more stability in your life, then it may be possible to start exploring how to process what has occurred.

MULTIPLE LOSSES

At times, multiple relationship losses may occur all at once—or you may experience a number of losses over a relatively short period of time. Both of these scenarios make it difficult to process grief. When you feel ready to start processing your losses, it can be beneficial to start with the easiest first and move through to the most difficult, working through the losses one at a time. Engaging a professional is likely to be beneficial in this instance. Each death or other significant loss needs to be respected and explored in the ways that feel right to you.

Losses that have not been processed are stored in your unconscious, and when you experience further loss these unprocessed losses can push to the surface, so that your reactions to a recent loss, even if it is a comparatively small one, may be more extreme than you would normally expect.

SUDDENNESS/UNEXPECTEDNESS

As a general rule, the more unexpected and sudden a loss, the greater the difficulty in coming to terms with it. This is in relation to one's own thinking and expectations, and also in relation to societal expectations. For example, a child dying is both personally and socially unexpected, since we see the natural progression of life being that parents die before their children. Losing a child is particularly difficult, no matter what their age.

A loved one becoming ill and dying within a short time frame is also sudden and unexpected, particularly when you have envisioned many years of togetherness and shared experiences. Accidents, natural disasters, and many other situations also involve these aspects of suddenness and unexpectedness. Trauma can often be attached to these experiences and multiple losses may occur, all of which need to be navigated.

Examples of sudden losses other than the unexpected death of a loved one would be having long-term employment suddenly terminated, or having your spouse or partner announce that they are leaving you, when you believed your relationship was stable.

Other possibilities that may include many aspects of both death and other losses include natural disasters such as floods, fires, earthquakes, cyclones, and other weather conditions. As these kinds of extreme weather events are becoming more frequent, there needs to be active planning and an awareness that the losses that accompany climate change will require exploring and processing.

Additionally, suddenness and unexpectedness are involved in any violent act, whether on a small scale or a large scale. Murder, homicide, terrorist acts, and war cause upheavals in society as well as in individual families. When on a large scale, this includes much trauma and many complications: not just in relation to immediate survival problems, but also over the long term—up to and including future generations. All this needs healing over the long term[43]. Whether this trauma and loss involves a particular ethnic or racial population, a subculture, a society or a country, it does not matter. All healing takes effort on the part of individuals and on the part of leaders.

TRAUMA

There are different ways of experiencing trauma. However, where there is a definite physical threat to one's survival, this is likely to be the most problematic and may result in symptoms of Post Traumatic Stress Disorder (PTSD).

VICARIOUS TRAUMA

Vicarious trauma doesn't threaten your existence, but instead involves other people's traumatic experiences, so that you have witnessed or heard stories about things that have happened to others, and this has affected your sense of security and safety in the world.

Where it comes to grief and loss, sometimes the loss may itself be traumatic or there may be traumatic aspects surrounding your loss. If you have traumatic experiences in your past then any aspects of these experiences may come up for you, so that processing your grief becomes more complicated or difficult. In this situation, where you feel you need extra support, it is very important to reach out and find the right person or people to empower you to release and resolve these extra layers of entanglement.

In the case where death isn't involved but there is an element of personal attack in some way, this can mean that trauma is experienced. For this reason, any situation that is threatening can give rise to trauma. Many different losses fall into this category, including natural disaster, being robbed, being physically attacked, and so on.

> If you have recently experienced a personal threat that has been traumatic and you have a sense of violation, then it is important to take steps to begin rebuilding your feelings of safety and security, within yourself and with the world. Explore finding and reaching out for the right support.

MANNER OF DEATH

Homicide or suicide may be very difficult to navigate. One question that may arise is 'why?' Sometimes, the answer to this question may not ever be known with certainty. If a random attack occurs, then it may not be possible to fully make sense of it.

Homicide and suicide are inherently traumatic. There is the physical violence, the suddenness and, in many cases, the unexpectedness. With suicide, self-recriminations and self-blame may be very large hurdles to process in the grieving process. Finding the body often adds an extra layer of trauma into the process. Where this specific trauma is processed first, it can be easier to begin processing the actual loss. However, it depends on your circumstances and access to support, as well as other factors.

Context also needs to be taken into account. These kinds of situations are most traumatic when family members and friends are involved.

SELF-ASSESSMENT OF COMPLICATIONS

Relating these factors to your own experience may indicate some aspect of your loss that could be eased through having extra support and ways of discussing and processing your loss. When a number of complications are present, having additional support and guidance can give you a pathway through the feelings of overwhelm.

Of course, it is still going to depend on you, your situation, the resources available to you, and your current level of support. Mostly, it depends on what kind of support you feel drawn to, what your interests are, and what you feel you need and require right now. Later chapters will explore these in more depth.

For now, if you feel unsure about anything and think you could do with some information and guidance, ask around for support.

YOUR GRIEVING PROCESS

Even if you do not have any factors that complicate your loss, there are still all the factors related to general loss, such as the strength of the relationship, how you interpret your loss in terms of your identity, roles, and expectations, alongside your thoughts and feelings about your future. For this reason, the context of the loss and the meaning you place on it may mean your grief is extremely intense. All this requires making sense of. Doing so consciously is best.

UNRESOLVED GRIEF

Unresolved grief can occur in a number of instances.

Firstly, if you have not been able to take yourself through the grieving process completely due to any of the factors and complications that can arise from a major loss, then you may still have unresolved grief. If you feel you are in such a situation, reaching out for professional support could be helpful.

Rituals and honouring your loss are also extremely important.

DISENFRANCHISED GRIEF

Disenfranchised grief can arise when your community, culture or society does not recognise that you have experienced a major loss. Examples of disenfranchised loss may include miscarriage, abortion, or separation from your children. There are many other circumstances where you may experience disenfranchised grief.

The important thing to realise in these cases is that you can create your own rituals that may be of benefit to your particular situation.

Again, don't leave it up to other people to control how you heal. Reach out and ask for support.

THE IMPACT OF OUR EXPECTATIONS

Expectations that we have for our lives may also give rise to grief when things don't turn out in the way we had hoped. Examples of this include:

- When a child has health issues/disabilities and you are a carer for them
- When a loved one suffers a life-changing accident
- When you suffer a life-changing accident
- Long illnesses and lingering deaths
- Chronic stress and anxiety

If you are in a caring role, it is very important to connect with organisations in your area that provide support.

CHECKLIST TO IMPROVE YOUR CLARITY

- Acknowledge that what you are feeling is grief
- Depending on context, there may or may not be an end point to your grieving process.
- It is often useful to have a sense of purpose in your life. If you have lost your sense of purpose, it can be recreated through exploration—or you may find a new sense of purpose.
- If the loss was expected, you may still experience great shock. For instance, with illness, there is always hope until the actual death. Anticipatory grief may not make the loss any easier to manage, or make the feelings less intense when the loss does occur.

THE NORMAL GRIEF STORM

A useful analogy for the experience of grief, particularly after a major loss, was put forward by Graham Fulton in 1989[44].

He describes *The Normal Grief Storm*, where people feel as though they are in a small boat on the ocean, being tossed around in a violent storm. There are three main components of The Normal Grief Storm.

1. The waves of emotion—and thoughts questioning whether you should be experiencing what you are feeling.
2. The winds of disturbed behaviour—including lack of energy, inability to concentrate, sleep disturbance, withdrawing, and dreaming.
3. The fog of disturbed thought processes—such as forgetfulness, disorientation, disorganised thinking, confusion, and preoccupation.

There is a great deal of difference between 'getting over' grief and living with it. It really depends on your loss and all its aspects. It is more likely that where close relationships are involved, then it can be better to see yourself living with it, since the grief itself may not go away. Living with grief means finding ways to accept your loss and creating memories that help keep you connected to your loss, so that your relationship with who or what has been lost still continues over time. This relationship may be in your mind and your heart.

In this chapter we have explored some different experiences of grief and some of the complications surrounding grief and loss. In the next chapter we will discuss realisations that can arise after the loss, and look at the significance of secondary losses.

CHAPTER 5 SUMMARY

Your grief journey is a very individual thing. The acute phase of grieving or mourning will depend on many factors, including:

- The kind of loss.
- The strength of the relationship.
- Personal factors, including your history, beliefs, and attachment style.
- Situational factors around the loss.
- Your unique coping styles.
- The unexpectedness of the loss.
- Any trauma or violence related to the loss.
- Whether the loss is personal or a wider community loss.
- The amount of support received.
- How much time and space is available to consciously process your grief.
- Your relationships with the people providing professional and personal support.

There may be many layers to unpack. Take it slowly and continue to move forward.

CHAPTER 6

SECONDARY LOSSES

Major losses will always be accompanied by secondary losses. These secondary losses will be very personal to you and will also be affected by what is going on around you, which may encompass your friends, family, community or the whole of humanity.

Loss can create feelings of anxiety and fear. By rising to the challenge of facing uncertainty, in the knowledge that you can explore new ways of being, behaving, and living, then it is possible to gain a clearer sense of self and an increased ability to see yourself as worthy and capable just as you are, regardless of status. In this way, personal growth and transformation is both possible and positive. These positive elements do not negate the grief. However, all life transitions present the opportunity to learn and grow.

Some secondary losses may be classified as temporary, while others may be permanent. In either case, it may be possible to find new sources that provide what was lost. If the loss is not recoverable, acceptance of your new situation on both a mental and an emotional level can be key to managing life better.

SECONDARY LOSSES THAT MAY FOLLOW A DEATH OR OTHER SIGNIFICANT LOSS:

- Roles
- Practical support
- Quality time
- Advice
- Bonding
- Love/relationship
- Future dreams/plans
- Future contact
- Companionship
- Physical presence
- Aspects of social life
- Friendship circles
- Aspects of lifestyle
- Changes within family relationships

These are just a few of the secondary losses. There may be additional secondary losses that are specific to your circumstances.

Sometimes, family ruptures can occur. Family members may have pre-existing issues or new issues may arise following a major loss. In either case, it can be very difficult to predict how family members are going to behave when they are grieving. For this reason, it is very helpful to have all the necessary legal documents in place, such as wills and power of attorney, so that sorting through possessions is not fraught with tension and anger. This is important in any situation where possessions need to be divided.

If there are difficult family relationships to begin with, these may be exacerbated by a death or other significant loss. However, family bonds can be made stronger following a loss.

The primary loss can mean that it may be difficult to make sense of your secondary losses until a little further along in your grief journey, so that you may realise them in a gradual way, in context of an event or situation that comes up. When your loss has been the death of someone close, the roles they played within your life may mean that you now need to become more independent or find other people who can give you support and advice.

RELATIONSHIP LOSSES

When Bernadette lost her partner, she found herself needing to do practical things such as changing light bulbs and putting the bins out, as well as being required to step into the role of managing relationships with mechanics and tradespeople regarding car and home maintenance. She also needed to take care of the finances, which was something her partner had previously managed.

Managing these kinds of everyday tasks falls under the umbrella of secondary losses.

It doesn't really matter how household chores are divided, if one person tended to do certain things, when they are no longer there it is necessary to either do it yourself, or find someone to do it for you. Relating this back to Worden's task theory, this is part of the task of readjusting to the world in which the deceased is missing. Working through what you need to do now means that you can gradually become more confident about managing independently.

After Alison lost her partner, she found that intense emotions arose around the loss of their future plans, from the holidays they had talked about going on, to simply spending quiet time together at home once the children had grown up and left. However, she surprised herself by being able to get her head around the finances that her partner had been so brilliant at managing, and made sure she looked after herself physically so that she was eating, sleeping and taking care of the house. Managing these practical secondary losses meant she started feeling a bit stronger over time, so that she was able to process the loss of the future she and her partner had planned.

Secondary losses may also include things you wish you could have said or done, and things you may regret having said or done. The loss of time to have conversations that might have created a greater sense of peace about the relationship also needs to be grieved.

In the case of a sudden loss, or in other circumstances where you were unable to be with the person at the time of death, it is important to make sense of this. Any feelings of guilt and regret need to be healed and released.

ASPECTS THAT MAY NEED CONSIDERATION FOR OTHER KINDS OF LOSSES INCLUDE:

Following the loss of employment – relationships with work colleagues, the feeling of being useful and valued, financial support and stability

Following the loss of your home and/or possessions through fire/flood/natural disaster/ acts of war/acts of violence/forced migration/ voluntary migration – sense of safety and security, survival issues, community, sense of place, sense of identity, sense of agency

Following the loss of a relationship/friendship/or following estrangement from family members – role, status, sense of place, sense of identity

Following the loss of health through accident/ illness/violence – sense of safety, sense of self, sense of identity, confidence, independence

Following the loss of someone who is a missing person – sense of safety, sense of certainty, confidence, trust

Following a financial loss/identity theft through being scammed or conned – sense of safety, sense of self, confidence, trust

Following personal trauma/violence – sense of safety, sense of self, confidence, trust

Climate Change Anxiety –a hoped-for future

This list is not comprehensive, but gives some insight into the secondary losses that can arise following significant losses and life events other than the death of a loved one.

In addition to significant losses and the secondary losses that arise from them, we all experience smaller losses that we may need to make sense of as well.

With smaller losses, we may not be as emotionally invested in what has been lost. For minor things, such as breaking a favourite vase, you might feel a bit upset or angry, but the feeling is not going to last for long. It is easier to explain the loss to yourself.

PERSONAL RESPONSIBILITY AND SENSE OF CONTROL

The experience of loss is often not a choice. When this is the case, the loss is something that happens *to* you. When you create a change in your life that is also accompanied by a loss, what is lost may be more easily explored and mourned for, because the change is something that has happened as the result of a choice you have made. For this reason, when losses occur outside of our control, we tend to experience a greater intensity of emotion and a greater sense of victimhood.

The best action here is to see this time as a challenge to get through. You can start very slowly and gradually, and begin taking responsibility for your emotions, thoughts, and behaviour.

It is important to have as much clarity as possible about where you are on your grief journey, and to understand where you are emotionally. It is no good trying to start this process until you feel completely ready. Just give yourself the time and space to go through the numb stage, to feel the disbelief, sadness, and any other emotions that arise. Allow yourself the time to grieve and to feel the pain of grief. Allow others to give you some care at this time, because you will need to apply your own self-care after what may feel like a very short time indeed, as your friends may begin to go back to their normal ways of being after a period of around three months.

Around the four-month mark is the time to begin to reach out for support. The numbness is likely to have worn off by this stage, and people who may have previously given you support are likely to have gone back to living their lives. You might be beginning to understand what your reality is and what has happened. At this time, your loss really starts to sink in.

If you feel ready to have some information that may be beneficial, or to explore particular counselling or support services, this is certainly the time to discuss your needs with others.

RELEASING THE SENSE OF FEELING STUCK

At times in life, we can feel that something could be better. That perhaps we could be feeling better, being in a better situation, or make our life better in some way. On these occasions, there is often a sense of not knowing what the options are, not understanding how to move forward, and not knowing what the catalyst for change would be. There can be a vague sense of wishing things were different, without having a sense or knowledge of how—or what—would create this difference. At these times, the main feeling can be that of being stuck.

When these kinds of feelings arise, what can make the difference is exploring the ways you are thinking and communicating. This is because change always starts with you and your mindset. Your mindset is how you think and communicate. In essence, your thoughts, attitudes, beliefs, and values make up your mindset. You have the power to change these aspects. You have control over yourself and how you communicate with others.

If you are finding relationships with others a bit uncertain or when conversations don't turn out the way you'd like, then one way of exploring what options you may have is to consider if you are immersing yourself in drama or running old behaviour programs from childhood. This relates to *the drama triangle*.

THE DRAMA TRIANGLE

The drama triangle can be a useful way of understanding the difficulties that sometimes arise in relationships. The drama triangle consists of three roles—the victim, the persecutor, and the rescuer.

Each role is part of a dysfunctional interaction that may be played out either within ourselves or with others. The victim role (poor me) relates to the child, the persecutor role (it's your fault) relates to the parent, and the rescuer role (let me help you) relates to a way of interacting with the victim that does not empower them, but instead keeps them dependent on the rescuer[45].

Generally speaking, when we take on one of these three roles, there is often a psychological 'reward'. The 'reward' may be to confirm a limiting belief such as 'I'm unworthy' or 'I'm better than you'.

Sometimes, people get stuck in patterns that were set in childhood and stay in these roles throughout their lives. However, it is healthier to jump out of the drama triangle and interact **adult-to-adult**.

In an adult-to-adult social interaction each person takes responsibility for themselves and doesn't blame others. There is logic and reasoning within the interaction and each person treats the other as an adult and as an equal.

If you find or feel that you cannot reach the adult-to-adult position at first, consider thinking about the drama triangle roles in a different way, as suggested in the conflict resolution book, *Everyone Can Win*[46], which reframes the victim as the learner, the persecutor as the teacher, and the rescuer as the mediator. All these roles are adult and equal.

HOW THE DRAMA TRIANGLE RELATES TO YOUR GRIEF JOURNEY

Following a loss, you may feel like a victim. Something very painful has happened to you, and as a result of this you may be feeling helpless.

Perhaps you are persecuting yourself for not doing things—all those 'what-ifs'.

Perhaps you are trying to be rescued, because it feels overwhelming to try and find a way through your grief on your own.

If you find you are taking on any of these roles, being self-compassionate and kind to yourself is a good way to step out of the triangle.

Sometimes it feels easier to stay in the triangle than to face the reality of your loss. Although it might not be easy to move forward in your life—in fact it might be amazingly difficult—it is possible.

For instance, by shifting the way you see yourself from being a victim to being a learner, you can begin to apply the information you gain from the people you find support from, and start to heal yourself.

By reframing the roles of victim, persecutor, and rescuer as learner, teacher, and mediator, you can:

- become stronger and more confident in the knowledge that you can manage life following your loss.
- gain self-empowerment as you take action to change your thoughts, feelings, and behaviours so that you can manage life better.

By continuing this process, you ensure that you are only taking responsibility for what you are *actually* responsible for—which is essentially yourself.

When stepping out of the drama triangle and into a place where your interactions are adult-to-adult, it is beneficial to be curious about what is happening and why you are experiencing particular feelings. The more you practice this, the better you get at it. As a result, any feelings of anger, disappointment, guilt, shame, bitterness, and so on—along with any associated thoughts—will lessen.

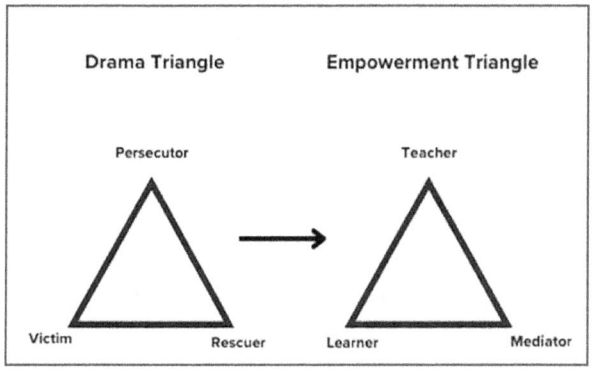

CHAPTER 6 SUMMARY

- All significant loss will be accompanied by secondary losses.
- Loss often touches our sense of identity, our roles, and our sense of place in the world.
- When you experience loss, you may feel like a victim.
- Feeling like a victim may be related to feeling you cannot create change in your life.
- Although grief does need sitting with and processing, the sooner you can start to take charge of yourself the better.
- When you feel ready, start noticing the things you are responsible for—yourself, your thoughts, your feelings, and your behaviours.
- See yourself as a learner rather than a victim.
- Find the people who may be able to act as teachers and guides to empower you to manage things better.

CHAPTER 7

EVERYDAY GRIEF

Grief may touch our everyday lives, even when we do not necessarily recognise it as such. This is because we often believe that grief needs to be very intense and related to a significant loss, rather than something that manifests as anxiety, regret or other less intense emotions.

When there is a community event that creates loss on any scale, we are able to come together and mourn that loss with others. This is an aspect of honouring and sharing in the losses of others. The personal impact that the loss has in our own lives doesn't matter. Because we are social beings, we come together and support those who are in deeper mourning.

We may also feel grief for individuals when they experience a significant loss. Even if you only know the person through their public life or media presence, you can still have a *felt connection* to them. Through connecting with others who are also grieving, there is a shared connection and honouring that takes place.

If you have a more personal connection to the person who has experienced a significant loss, then honouring their loss acknowledges the relationship you have with them. This can be healing for you, as well as for the person who has experienced the significant loss.

THE POWER OF RITUALS

Any kind of ritual allows us to honour our loss and can help create feelings of completion and closure in our hearts and minds.

How we view closure around death is guided by our cultural customs. These customs can be a very powerful aspect of the mourning process. Different cultures have different mourning rituals, relating to behaviour, the length of the mourning period, and so on. It can be helpful for everyone to take part in the rituals, because they impart a sense of involvement and belonging, which is one way they can bring a sense of closure. Rituals around death also memorialise the person or people who have been lost, and can therefore help to increase emotional acceptance.

If you have not been able to participate in the rituals as would be usual for you, all is not lost. This is because although rituals usually occur in reality, and rituals take place in particular places, your mind cannot tell the difference between what happens in real life and what you imagine. Thus, you can actually create your own ritual to give yourself this sense of completion. Make your imagined ritual as real as possible, taking yourself through all the details of this experience. Include all your senses, so that you imagine what you would see, hear, feel, and so on. Imagine it all the way through from start to finish. This should make some difference to how you feel about it.

VICARIOUS TRAUMA

People who are present at the scene of accidents, crimes or other traumatic events may experience vicarious trauma. This term is used when a person becomes traumatised, even though their personal safety has not been threatened. The quantity of incidents that people are exposed to may have a deleterious effect on their mental health. First responders are high on the list of those who can experience vicarious trauma, as well as being at risk of experiencing personal threat and trauma.

People supporting those who have experienced trauma may become burnt out if they do not have proper breaks, sufficient rest, and effective ways of processing the things they hear, see, and feel.

WAR AND GLOBAL ISSUES

In Australia, we are lucky not to be involved in any major global wars at this time. However, many residents and citizens of Australia will know people who are living in a country that is experiencing hardship, including war. Much anxiety and concern may be experienced for loved ones who are in these situations.

If you have friends or family who are in this situation, you can:

- Maintain your own physical, emotional, mental and spiritual balance. Consuming too much traumatic news can have a deleterious effect on your health and wellbeing[47].

- Use reliable sources that are informative in relation to what is happening.

- If there is action you can take that may be useful, which doesn't prevent or inhibit you from keeping your own life on track, this might be something to do.

- Getting together with others in similar circumstances may provide a level of social support.

GRIEF SITUATIONS ON AN EVERYDAY LEVEL

Some situations that do not fit into the bracket of being a significant loss may be seen in a continuum on the pathway towards such a label. It can be beneficial to work out a strategy that helps you when difficult situations or emotions arise.

Firstly, are you using active coping strategies? If not, incorporating these strategies may be of benefit. Secondly, consider how you see your identity and whether you believe you are able to make choices about your life, or if you feel you live your life in reaction to others and whatever occurs around you.

In other words, are you taking responsibility for yourself? If so, you should be perceiving yourself as your own change agent.

It is absolutely ok to occasionally see yourself as a victim, providing you recognise this perspective quickly so that you can get back on track and take responsibility for yourself and your life choices.

If you feel that no actions you can take will create change within yourself or your life, then you are seeing yourself as a victim of circumstances. This means you see yourself as being swayed around by life and by other people. With this kind of thinking, you are abdicating responsibility for yourself. You *do* have the ability to create change—at least in terms of the ways you think, behave, and feel about things.

EXPLORING RELATIONSHIP PATTERNS

Following a significant loss, after some time has passed, if you feel stuck and unable to create a life for yourself that has meaning and purpose, it may be of benefit to look back over your life and explore your relationship with yourself and your relationships with others.

Only **you** can change yourself and your life. Until you are able to recognise this and take action, you will continue to repeat the patterns of your past. This applies to relationships, and also to any issues in your life that you may not find easy to manage. For instance, you may find it difficult to be assertive or you may be a people-pleaser.

By looking at your life patterns, particularly in terms of relationships and how you manage difficult situations, you can learn more about yourself. Many people are not taught how to observe themselves or how to manage important things such as emotions and self-regulation. It can take time to learn how to do these things.

By stepping back from yourself and observing what is happening, you can begin to improve your self-awareness and gain clarity about the best coping strategies to use in order to improve your relationship with yourself and your relationships with others. For instance, are you proactive? If so, then you are planning ahead and thinking of the possible consequences that may result from actions you take and behaviours you engage in.

If you are reactive rather than proactive, you are only looking at what is in front of you. It is worth considering if this works for you.

Daily life may require a combination of being proactive and also responding to unexpected, unplanned situations and events that arise. It is far better to be proactive about major life events, and to have a number of strategies and plans available in your tool box to use when needed when you need to respond to unexpected situations.

Having a game plan really is practical and useful. If you are also able to be flexible and resilient in the process, your results and outcomes are likely to be more positive. This means you will be able to manage many different situations in ways that allow you to be true to yourself.

LIFE SITUATIONS AND LOSS

Occasionally, what we expect in life does not happen as we would like. Sometimes this may not be our fault, but due to circumstances beyond our control. On one level, this is just life. Life can be uncertain, and many factors have an effect on our world.

What is to be done in these circumstances? We like to have stability and certainty in our lives. Since we cannot be in control of what is happening around us and can only really affect what is within us, our perception of how we live, alongside our attitudes, values, and behaviours, make the most difference in our lives. If we attend to ourselves, then those people we associate with may be affected too, which can cause a ripple effect, so that those who are affected may affect other people in their lives. In this way, it may be possible to affect wider change by being true to ourselves.

We know that significant loss often sends out ripples, because many people are touched in some way by that loss.

YOUR LIFE VALUES

In her book, *The Top Five Regrets of the Dying,* Bronnie Ware suggests that when it comes down to the wire, people don't value things such as status, how much money they made, or even what they achieved [48].

Most often, the regrets of the dying relate to not having lived their life in particular ways. These included:

- not having the courage to be true to themselves
- not working purposefully, even if they'd worked hard
- not expressing their feelings to others
- not staying in touch with their friends
- not allowing themselves to be happier
- not having lived in the present

HOW CAN YOU ENSURE YOU DO NOT HAVE THESE REGRETS?

When you lose someone or something that gave meaning to your life, your mission is to find new meaning. It is possible for you to discover who you are now, and to live a life that is true to **you**. By taking action, you can discover how you want to move forward in your life.

RELIGIOUS AND SPIRITUAL BELIEFS

Your beliefs about death and life after death can impact how you see your life, your expectations of life, and what kinds of things you think you should be doing within your life.

It could be that your loss experiences have shaken or shattered your beliefs. It is not uncommon for people who have experienced a significant loss to question beliefs they have held for many years. When you find yourself questioning past interpretations of experiences and feelings you might be surprised. If you find that your beliefs and feelings are no longer aligned, this can create a crisis of faith.

Alternatively, your beliefs may have been strengthened. Whether your experience of loss strengthens your faith or causes you to question your beliefs, you may find that you are brought to a place that helps you to make sense of your world and your new reality.

Whether you define your spiritual life as a sense of wonder in nature, a sense of oneness, or a belief in God or another higher power, your spiritual life has meaning for you. Regardless of your spiritual beliefs, you need to live your life to the fullest, in the present moment, being your authentic self.

This may mean disregarding all those 'shoulds' in your life, and being happy with going along your own path. However, in whatever case, it does mean living true to you and what you feel is important.

CASE STUDIES - SPIRITUAL EXPERIENCES FOLLOWING SIGNIFICANT LOSS

Those who have lost loved ones, particularly through death, may experience vivid dreams and have experiences that defy logic.

Wendy had a difficult marriage and separated from her husband. Following the separation, their son, Richard, went to live with his father. Three months later, Richard committed suicide. Wendy was devastated by his death, and this caused her to doubt her faith. Two weeks after Richard's death, he visited her in spirit. He smiled and spoke to her, saying, 'Mum, I'm at peace. Now you be at peace too.' He smiled again, she blinked, and he was gone. This experience allowed her to understand that Richard was okay, which restored her faith.

***

When my father was dying, I drove to my parents' home, arriving the day before he died. I was able to spend time at his bedside, just holding his hand and being there with him. The following day my mum, my siblings, and I sat with him and sent him our love. I recognised the moment he died and his spirit left his body. I burst into tears and simultaneously felt an uplifting joy in my heart. This was not my joy, but my father's. It still touches me now.

***

Many of my grief support group members have their own stories of feeling deeply connected to their loved ones, and are thankful for having had those experiences. Spiritual or not, these experiences help to bring comfort and create a sense that things are okay.

EXPLORING SPIRITUALITY

- ❖ Imagine moving beyond your childhood conditioning, including the behaviours, beliefs, and thought patterns that you learned in your formative years.

- ❖ Imagine that changing the way you approach life is less about willpower and more about seeing your brain as your tool that you can reprogram, so that you can move away from ways of thinking and being that no longer serve you, and allow yourself to be who you really want to be.

- ❖ Imagine you are a spiritual being having a physical experience, and that you can see your time in this world as an opportunity to make some kind of positive difference—however big or small that difference may be.

- ❖ Imagine life is a series of challenges that we learn to meet, so that we can grow in strength on emotional, mental, and spiritual levels. These challenges may relate to the things you find most difficult in life.

- ❖ Imagine there is a higher power, and that all religions have the essence of this power, but not all the actuality.

EXPLORING SPIRITUALITY

❖ Imagine you have your own support community in spirit, consisting of your passed loved ones, your spirit guide, and other spirit beings who are there encouraging you and supporting you as much as they are able.

❖ Imagine the person you love who has died is with you, at least for as long as needed. What difference does this make to how you think about them now?

❖ Imagine that you have lived many lives with those you feel closely connected to, and that you will meet them again and continue other lives together.

THE IMPORTANCE OF DREAMS

Our loved ones may appear to us in dreams, either to give us messages or to show us that they are okay. Because our brains are powerful processors and dreams serve multiple purposes, it may be possible to harness your dreams. You can train your brain to do many things, and remembering dreams is no exception.

For a while after my father died, my brain was grappling with the idea that he was gone. I dreamed of him being dead and then coming back younger and healthier. I dreamed of him being sick rather than dead, and I dreamed that he was healthy and still alive. All these different combinations were presented to me. At the same time as my unconscious mind was processing what had happened, I was also processing my loss consciously. After some time, my conscious and unconscious mind came to the same conclusion about the person my father was, and how I wanted to remember him.

Although I rarely dream of my father now, I do keep a dream journal in which I write down the dreams I remember. It is worthwhile making sense of your dreams if you are interested in this area.

There are a number of different ways you can use and interpret your dreams. Go with the ones that feel best for you. It can be an interesting way to utilise your creativity to provide you with food for thought.

CLIMATE CHANGE FUTURES

Now that climate change is bringing more extreme weather conditions and more frequent natural disasters, there is a greater need to address how people caught up in the middle of these events can be more resilient. We all need to consider how to manage in a changing world. Much grief is likely to be involved.

Facing an uncertain future is already causing anxiety, and there has been a great deal of discussion about what could happen and what we should be doing about it. Many people feel powerless. Many people want to do something to make a difference, but don't know what will work best.

Preparation may be useful. Your personal preparation could include developing a high level of flexibility and resilience.

CHAPTER 7 SUMMARY

- Grief may touch our lives on an everyday level.
- Rituals are powerful healing tools that can help us find some closure.
- Trauma issues may be experienced both first-hand and vicariously.
- Sometimes things don't work out as you expect or hope. This is also a form of grief.
- Exploring themes and patterns in your life can be helpful.
- Finding meaning and purpose is of great importance.
- There are actions that can be taken to reduce regrets and to live a fulfilled life.
- Grief can change how we see our religious and spiritual practices.
- Climate Change grief is becoming more prevalent.

CHAPTER 8

WHERE ARE YOU RIGHT NOW?

Assessing where you are in your grief journey takes a certain amount of self-reflection and self-awareness. A number of factors can improve or impede your willingness to consciously explore any feeling of being 'stuck' in pain, as well as impacting on whether or not you feel able to seek outside support to alleviate the loneliness and feelings of isolation that grief may bring.

While there are both helpful and unhelpful ways of managing and coping with what comes up for you during the grieving process, it needs to be acknowledged that whatever you have been doing that has allowed you to work through your grief in the best way you can has been right for you up to now.

With the benefit of hindsight, there may be some different methods, behaviours, ways of thinking, or actions that you feel may have had a more positive outcome. However, we do the best we can with the information we have at the time.

One important point to note is that *only you* can do your own grieving. Sometimes we just need to sit with our grief for a while. However, if it gets too overwhelming, it might be time to do something else and adopt other strategies.

The aspects discussed below are predominantly things that may be difficult and which may create delays in your healing process.

UNCERTAINTY

We all like to have a reasonable level of dependability and reliability within our life circumstances. We prefer not to have shocks or sudden changes in our lives, and we like to be able to rely on those who love and support us. In this way, we feel safe and secure, and experience greater levels of happiness and harmony. Any uncertainty, whether it is in areas such as employment, personal safety, financial security, relationships, or health, is very difficult to live with. It can be very stressful to experience uncertainty, and may prevent the sense that there can be any resolution to painful experiences.

Where a loved one goes missing, this uncertainty

may last for many years. Not knowing whether a loved one or family member is alive or not is likely to be extremely difficult. When family members are estranged, if there is still some level of communication with other family members, it may be possible to develop an outlook that enables you to understand the situation, so that the pain may not be as intense. There can be possibilities of finding ways of managing this hole in your life, either at the time or at a later date. Sometimes, if you push your feelings down, they may still need to be explored later.

Uncertainty can also come into play when it comes to health. Even when a loved one is ill and has been ill for a long time, and even if we believe we have already grieved for them because we know they will not recover from the illness, it is often still a shock when they die.

Having some time to prepare for a loved one's death can be helpful, but it does not take away the shock when they die.

If you are ill or have an accident, then depending on your normal level of health, there are possibilities of recovering. For some chronic conditions, there could be options available that help to create a better quality of life over the long term.

TIME FRAMES

The grieving process occurs over time, and the amount of time will be unique to you. However, if quite a long time has passed and you still feel that you are stuck in the pain of grief, it may be beneficial to seek professional help or a higher level of support from friends and family.

Whether you reach out to others in the days following a significant loss or whether it is weeks, months or years later, is absolutely fine. You set the time frame. The timing is all about when you feel ready and wish to change the intensity of emotion, the feelings of uncertainty, or the level of loneliness and isolation you are experiencing.

THE GAP BETWEEN WHERE YOU ARE NOW AND WHERE YOU'D LIKE TO BE

There is often a gap between where we are and where we'd like to be.

However, this gap may become a great deal more obvious when we experience a loss, go through some kind of life transition, or have unexpected events occur in our lives that force us to look at who we are and where we are in our lives.

When death and loss are around us, we may start to question our own mortality, because we suddenly see that life is so precious and can be taken away at any time. The best time to act is always now. If we continue to put things off, it may be too late to live a truly fulfilling life. Any time you start to question your life, if you allow yourself to enter into this space there can be gold waiting for you within.

A GIFT

Through exploring and delving into your experience of loss you may discover a gift. Every loss has gifts attached. These do not have to be exactly related in a direct line to who or what you lost. The gift may be totally unrelated, but by giving yourself permission to explore and think deeply about yourself and your life, along with the meanings of your losses, you create the space and time to strike gold. The gift may be self-transformation and a more secure sense of self, or it might be something totally different.

We all have potential for expressing our personal talents and gifts to support and empower others and to create a better world. This does not have to be a huge endeavour: finding what you can do for yourself, your friends, your family or your community are all wonderful ways of exploring how you can use your gifts.

There could be opportunities to communicate in better ways with family members and to forge more secure relationships. Sometimes families become fractured following a significant loss, and other times closer relationship bonds can be formed.

The gift that follows a loss might be that you now have the freedom to do something you have always wanted to do. It might be that you discover a new passion or it might be that you find a way of honouring your loved one by taking up a cause.

WHAT ABOUT THE GAP?

If there is a gap between where you are now and where you want to be in your life, you now have the opportunity to move towards what you want. Whatever inner vision you have for yourself, you can create a new version of you.

This gap may feel small or it may feel as though it is a very wide chasm. If you take things one step at a time and explore what you would like to be different, both within yourself and outside yourself, then you can make a start on finding your own unique pathway to healing.

GOAL SETTING

Set goals for what you would like to be different. Be realistic, so that your goals are achievable. Remember that you cannot change others. You can only change yourself.

Ask yourself what you want. This could be:

- to feel more peace
- to find more effective coping strategies
- to explore who you are now
- to make sense of your loss
- to feel less pain
- to feel less overwhelmed

ASKING FOR SUPPORT – DIFFERENT OPTIONS

- **Individual Counselling**

  A psychologist or counsellor who has trained in grief and loss or has experience in this area will likely be able to support you in navigating your grieving process.

- **Group Counselling**

  A face-to-face grief support group can be extremely useful in enabling you to know that you are not alone, and to discover the support of others who are in a similar situation of loss. It does take some time for grief to be processed, and a group can kick-start this process.

- **Online Support**

  There is a range of possibilities for online

connections and support, and online programs that may be appropriate for your needs. These include:

1. Forums and groups where you can share your situation and converse with others in similar circumstances. Take steps to ensure these are genuine groups run by genuine people who have the right training or experience

2. Websites that provide information and resources

3. Podcasts you can listen to—either to help you understand your grief process better, or to distract yourself as needed

4. Webinars that you can access at low cost or free of charge

5. Online grief programs you can do in your own time and at your own pace.

- **Reading Books**

If you enjoy reading, there are some very good books by people who have experienced loss and have written about how they came to be transformed by their grief and how they underwent this transformation.

ASSESSING WHAT MAY WORK FOR YOU

When exploring which modalities and processes may work for you, some aspects that you may wish to consider are:

- How much support you feel you need and what type of support you want
- What type of situation you are most comfortable in
- Whether you would prefer talking to one other person or a group of people
- Whether you would prefer talking in person or online
- The amount you want to reveal about yourself and how safe you feel about doing this
- Any safety issues in relation to your physical or emotional needs
- Any confidentiality issues which would impede the process of sharing your story. You may prefer to share with a professional rather than friends or family, since a professional will keep confidentiality
- The kind of professional you would like to support you. In this respect, it is important to consider:
  * Matching values

* Matching beliefs (or at least acceptance of one another's beliefs)
* Qualifications and specialisations
* What the costs would be, and what your financial situation will allow
* Your geographical location, whether the kinds of therapy/counselling/experiential practices you are drawn to are available in your area, and your willingness to be flexible about finding what will suit your needs, either in person or online.
* Your assessment of your needs—taking into account your circumstances and situation

ASSESSING YOUR NEEDS

Consider what results or outcomes you are likely to achieve through the particular kinds of support you feel drawn to. The importance of exploring this cannot be overstated.

If you do nothing when you have assessed yourself as needing some structure and support in your healing journey, then you are likely to remain where you are right now. It is through taking action that you will create change. It may be scary. It may be something you have never done before. That is absolutely fine. Reaching out for support when you need it is a strength, and by doing so you will find a greater sense of belonging and peace in your life. If you feel you could benefit from support, have courage and reach out.

In relation to your self-assessment, there are also considerations regarding the kinds of support you feel are appropriate for you. If you feel that you are in crisis, then perhaps a short-term intervention is needed. If you feel this is best for you right now, there are phone services available such as Lifeline. There may be other similar services in your local area.

There are some crisis lines that may refer on to other services or have additional services of their own that you can access.

A referral may be made to a psychologist or other specialist through a medical practitioner. In Australia, a mental health care plan enables referral to a psychologist with a number of sessions available at reduced rates.

Additionally, there are counsellors and other practitioners who can support you and provide a space for you to start to heal. Although counsellors do not charge as much as psychologists, it is important to find out if they are accredited with a reputable counselling association, and to ensure they have trained in the area you want support in, such as grief and loss. In Australia, there is The Australian Counselling Association (ACA) and PACFA (Psychotherapy and Counselling Federation of Australia) amongst other associations.

In this chapter I have described ways and means of finding the right support for you and things to consider in this area. The next chapter will delve even deeper into Your Pathway to Self-Healing.

CHAPTER 8 SUMMARY

- Take responsibility for finding the right services to help and support you.
- Ask around, get referrals, and go with what feels right.
- Ask questions, and if you are interested in a particular modality or way of working on yourself find those who can provide this service.
- Consider whether you require crisis support, short-term support, or medium-term to longer-term support.
- Consider access, your financial situation, and other resources you have, both within yourself, in your local area, and at a wider distance.
- When you are considering what your needs are, you may wish to ask people around you for recommendations for services and individuals that may be able to provide you with appropriate help and support.
- Having looked at the gap between where you are and where you'd like to be, think about what might empower you to progress towards your goal.
- How far you progress will depend on a number of factors, including your willingness to make changes in your life.

CHAPTER 9

FINDING YOUR OWN PATHWAY TO PEACE AND PURPOSE

How do you tell if someone can support you?

How can you know if a particular form of support will work for you?

How can you find a sense of purpose in your life again?

These questions are meaningful and valuable to ask yourself and anyone you are considering contacting in order to help determine if they are going to be of help to you.

There needs to be a fit between what your vision of your future looks like (as you want it to be) and what anyone is able to provide. These things need to match in your mind. There needs to be a match of values and ways of working together that create a meaningful and positive relationship between you and the other person.

It is the relationship between you and the other person that makes everything work in counselling, coaching or any kind of professional relationship where the aim is for you to reach a goal or health outcome[49].

When we look back over our lives, we can often identify when having someone to talk with in a counselling, coaching or a mentorship situation—providing knowledge and support, and presenting us with ideas and options—could have been exactly what we needed. Hindsight is, of course, 100%.

It is often when we cannot identify what it is we need and feel that we have to push through and manage by ourselves that we either remain stuck or take a long time to work through painful emotions before we find ourselves again.

In order to escape this trap, there are some points to note:

- When you feel something is missing and are undecided, unsure, and uncertain, this is the time to reach out to seek support.

- Consider how much of your time is spent feeling isolated and alone. This may be emotionally, mentally or physically. If you find that you feel isolated and alone a great deal of the time, reaching out for support may help.

- Investigate what services may be available to you by asking friends, family, and your local and online communities for recommendations.

- Follow where your interest is. If you feel inspired by some method, technique or modality, find out more.

- Be hopeful that you can find the people and services that will help empower you to get where you want to be.

- To find the right match, explore how someone usually works. Think about how what they say makes you feel. If you feel positive about how they usually work, then this is a sign to explore more deeply.

- Once you've established that you feel positive about the way someone works, have a conversation with them. This can help give you some idea of what the fit will be like.

- Have a trial session. It is possible that after an initial session, you realise that it is not quite right for you. This is ok. Sometimes it is worth talking to the person you are seeking support from, because there may be some miscommunication that can be resolved. If you find this isn't the case, look for someone else.

- Always take responsibility for your own healing. Don't expect anyone to wave a magic wand. You need to do the work. Healing does take effort. The more consciously you put the effort in, the more progress you will make.

Many people who have experienced a loss that is not complicated by some of the more difficult factors discussed in this book are able to manage on their own, with perhaps just a bit of information from books, podcasts or other resources.

If you have assessed yourself as needing further support, then consider what would suit your needs best—taking into account your personal situation and access to resources.

If you feel you need extra support then don't hesitate to start your self-healing journey—wherever that is and through whoever you feel is the right person or program for you. Taking action to start your healing journey *now* will make the difference.

CHAPTER 9 SUMMARY

- Finding the right professional or services for you may require some exploration on your part.
- Ask the people who might support you about their professional status, training, and how they will work with you.
- Find out if they are a good match for you by having a conversation with them.
- If it feels right and you like the person, this can be a really good start to a successful and productive professional relationship.
- Research shows that what matters most for healing is the relationship between you and your health professional.

CONCLUSION

When writing *A Practical Guide for Grief & Loss*, the aim was to provide a book that was inclusive, and which discussed the process of healing in a way that was accessible and easy to read. In line with this aim, the book is fairly short, even though the subject is very complex and broad.

The most important points to understand are that grief is normal and universal, and that everyone grieves in their own unique way. The grieving process is not limited to loss through death, but encompasses many different life experiences.

Those losses we experience as major losses are intense for us, and it is these significant losses that we need to pay a high level of attention to in the processing of our new reality. This is the case no matter whether you have experienced loss through death or whether you are going through a life change such as emigration, involvement in a natural disaster, retirement or divorce. To some extent, making a decision to change yourself and then taking action to do so, allows you to see the change and those losses involved as a challenge to rise to. When loss occurs and there is no sense of control over what has happened, your inner world is more greatly impacted. The patterns in your brain that have helped you negotiate life up to this time become disrupted, and through processing your loss and making sense of your new reality, you begin to find your way onto a new pathway. This journey may include finding a new purpose.

All kinds of loss need processing, whether or not this is understood or acknowledged by anyone. While your community, society or culture may not realise this need, it is critical that as individuals we take responsibility for our own mental, emotional, and physical health and explore how we can grow and become the best versions of ourselves. It is a vision we may dream of or glimpse in moments of inspiration, but we often do not act on the vision. When we experience a major loss, and certainly when death touches us in some form, we may begin facing the idea of our own mortality. This exploration provides a golden opportunity to start embracing what we really want out of life. We can then begin the journey that takes us on our self-healing pathway to peace and purpose.

I hope that reading this book has inspired you to continue on your self-healing journey and that you can fulfil your own vision for who you want to be.

Love does not die, and nor does the hope for a better future. The only way to create a better future is to take action in the present. Each act of self-care and self-compassion is another step on the journey, another way of taking responsibility for your own healing. Added together, these steps create a huge difference over time.

I wish you all the best in finding your unique self-healing pathway.

Yours in healing,

Diana Hutchison

REFERENCES

CHAPTER 1

1 Kessler, D. (2019) *Finding meaning: The sixth stage of grief.* London: Rider.

2 Davis, D.L. (2023) 'As you grieve your brain redraws its neural map. https://www.psychologytoday.com/us/blog/laugh-cry-live/202303/as-you-grieve-your-brain-redraws-its-neural-map. Accessed 30/3/2023

3 Worden, J.W. (2010) *Grief counselling and grief therapy: A handbook for the mental health practitioner.* London: Routledge.

4 (No date) *Mental health impact of covid 19.* Available at: https://www.aihw.gov.au/getmedia/6e2c41a8-d849-44ea-ab16-6e7d75503a14/mental-health-impact-of-covid-19.pdf.aspx (Accessed: 28 February 2024).

5 Bowlby, J. (1969) Attachment and Loss. Penguin:UK.

6 Hughes, Dan (2013) *8 Keys to Building Your Best Relationships (8 Keys to Mental Health).* WW Norton & Company: New York.

CHAPTER 2

7 Kübler-Ross, E. (1970) *On death and dying.* New York: Macmillan.

8 Kübler-Ross, D. and Kessler, E. (2014) *On grief and grieving: Finding the meaning of grief through the five stages of loss*. London, UK: Simon & Schuster.

9 Kessler, D. (2022) Grief Summit April 28th 2022: *Counseling and Treatment Tools for the Changing Face of Grief and Loss* Online Webinar. Attended personally.

10 Kessler, D. (2019) *Finding meaning: The sixth stage of grief*. London: Rider.

11 Bowlby J. (1969) Attachment and Loss. Penguin:UK.

12 Worden, J.W. (2010) *Grief counselling and grief therapy: A handbook for the mental health practitioner*. London: Routledge.

13 Stroebe, M. and Schut, H. (1999) 'The Dual Process Model of coping with bereavement: Rationale and description', *Death Studies*, 23(3), pp. 197–224. doi:10.1080/074811899201046.

14 Maté, G. (2019) *When the body says no: The cost of Hidden Stress*. Brunswick, Victoria, Australia: Scribe.

15 Rankin, L. (2013) *Mind over Medicine: Scientific Proof That You Can Heal yourself*. Hay House:U.S.A.

16 Maté, G. (2019) *When the body says no: The cost of Hidden Stress*. Brunswick, Victoria, Australia: Scribe.

17 Kessler, D. (2019) *Finding meaning: The sixth stage of grief*. London: Rider

CHAPTER 3

18 Tonkin, L. (1996) *Growing around grief: another way of looking at grief and recovery*, Bereavement Care vol 15, 1996, issue 1 (Accessed: 28 February 2024).

19 *Locus of control* (no date) *Julian Rotter, Personality Theories, Internal, and External - JRank Articles*. Available at: https://psychology.jrank.org/pages/387/Locus-Control.html (Accessed: 28 February 2024).

20 Van der Kolk, B. (2014) *The body keeps the score: Brain, mind, and body in the transformation of trauma*. New York: Viking.

21 Ferguson, S. (2022) *Top 10 stressors in life and why*, Psych Central. Available at: https://psychcentral.com/stress/top-10-life-stressors-that-can-trigger-anxiety#top-10-life-stressors (Accessed: 28 February 2024).

22 Maté, G. (2019) *When the body says no: The cost of Hidden Stress*. Brunswick, Victoria, Australia: Scribe.

23 *Broken heart syndrome* (2023) *Mayo Clinic*. Available at: https://www.mayoclinic.org/diseases-conditions/broken-heart-syndrome/symptoms-causes/syc-20354617#:~:text=Most%20people%20who%20have%20broken%20heart%20syndrome%20quickly%20recover%20and,heart%20syndrome%20can%20cause%20death. (Accessed: 17 April 2024).

24 Hay, Louise L. (1984) *You Can Heal Your Life*. Specialist Publications: Australia.

25 Hay, Louise L. (1984) *You Can Heal Your Life*. Specialist Publications: Australia.

CHAPTER 4

26 Van der Kolk, B. (2014) *The Body Keeps the Score: Mind, Brain and Body in the Transformation of Trauma*. Penguin Books, Random House:UK:

27 Rankin, L. (2013) *Mind over medicine*. S.I.: Hay House.

28 Mlodinow, L. (2023) *Emotional the new thinking about feelings*. London: Penguin Books Ltd.

29 Delbrige, A. (1982) *The concise macquarie dictionary*. Lane Cove: Doubleday.

30 Catherine Moore, P. (2024) *What is the negativity bias and how can it be overcome?*, PositivePsychology.com. Available at: https://positivepsychology.com/3-steps-negativity-bias/ (Accessed: 17 April 2024).

31 Mlodinow, L. (2023) *Emotional the new thinking about feelings*. London: Penguin Books Ltd.

32 Mlodinow, L. (2023) *Emotional the new thinking about feelings*. London: Penguin Books Ltd.

33 Mlodinow, L. (2023) *Emotional the new thinking about feelings*. London: Penguin Books Ltd.

34 Haidt, J. (2020) *The righteous mind: Why good people are divided by politics and religion*. Vancouver, B.C.: Langara College.

35 Jeremy Sutton, Ph.D. (2024) *5+ benefits of positive emotions on psychological wellbeing, PositivePsychology.com*. Available at: https://positivepsychology.com/benefits-of-positive-emotions/ (Accessed: 28 February 2024).

36 Kuppens, P., Realo, A., Diener, E.(2008) *The role of positive and negative emotions in life satisfaction judgment across nations, Journal of personality and social psychology*. Available at: https://pubmed.ncbi.nlm.nih.gov/18605852/ (Accessed: 28 February 2024).

CHAPTER 5

37 *Emotional and physical pain activate similar brain regions* (no date) *Psychology Today*. Available at: https://www.psychologytoday.com/au/blog/body-sense/201204/emotional-and-physical-pain-activate-similar-brain-regions#:~:text=When%20people%20feel%20emotional%20pain,and%20the%20anterior%20cingulate%20cortex. (Accessed: 17 April 2024).

38 Frumkin, M.R., Haroutounian, S., Rodebaugh, T.L. (2020) *Examining emotional pain among individuals with chronic physical pain: Nomothetic and idiographic approaches, Journal of psychosomatic research*. Available at: https://pubmed.ncbi.nlm.nih.gov/32622183/ (Accessed: 17 April 2024).

39 Gedlin, E.T. (1978) *Focusing*. Bantam Books: New York

40 Mlodinow, L. (2023) *Emotional: the new thinking about feelings*. London: Penguin Books Ltd.

41 Stanisławski, K. (2019) *The coping circumplex model: An integrative model of the structure of coping with stress, Frontiers in psychology.* Available at: https://www.ncbi.nlm.nih.gov/pmc/articles/PMC6476932/ (Accessed: 18 April 2024).

42 Maslow, A.H. (no date) *Maslow, A. H. (1942). the dynamics of psychological security-insecurity. journal of personality, 10, 331-344. - references - scientific research publishing.* Available at: https://www.scirp.org/(S(351jmbntvnsjt1aadkposzje))/reference/ReferencesPapers.aspx?ReferenceID=2118174 (Accessed: 29 February 2024).

43 Neuroscience News (2015) *Inheriting trauma: Holocaust survivors pass trauma to their children's genes, Neuroscience News.* Available at: https://neurosciencenews.com/epigenetics-trauma-transmission-2502/ (Accessed: 29 February 2024).

44 Fulton, Graham (1989). The normal grief storm: a model for understanding grief and loss. In National Association for Loss and Grief (ed.), *Proceedings of the Sixth National Conference*, National Association for Loss and Grief, Melbourne, 49-57. Cited by D. Morawetz, in What Works in Grief Counselling: US Evidence and Australian Experience. Grief Matters (2007) 8 pages – 1-8.

CHAPTER 6

45 Karpman, Stephen B. (2014) *"Ä Game Free Life" – The definitive book on the Drama Triangle and Compassion Triangle.* Drama Triangle Publications: USA

46 Cornelius, H. & Faire, S. (2006) *Everyone can Win: Responding to Conflict Constructively.* (2nd Ed) Simon & Schuster: Sydney

Note: These authors suggest a transfer from the drama triangle to a dynamic empowerment circle rather than a direct triangle to triangle translation. I think it is easier to understand and explain it however in a direct translation. Please see the original book for more details.

47 Benson, T. (2023) *It's time to log off*, *Wired*. Available at: https://www.wired.com/story/doomscrolling-bad-news-mental-health/#:~:text=Price%20says%20ingesting%20a%20lot,history%20of%20experiencing%20those%20conditions. (Accessed: 02 March 2024).

CHAPTER 7

48 Ware, Bronnie (2019) *The Top Five Regrets of the Dying: A life transformed by the Dearly Departing.* Hay House: Australia

CHAPTER 9

49 Morawetz, D. (2007) What Works in Grief Counselling: US Evidence and Australian Experience. *Grief Matters* 8 pages – 1-8.

ABOUT THE AUTHOR

Diana Hutchison is an author, counsellor and coach whose life-long passion for self-development has led her to create a series of books in the self-help genre. Being drawn towards understanding multiple ways and modalities, she sought to create meaning for herself and her life which has meant that her unique holistic approach explores all levels of being: physical, mental, emotional and spiritual, leading to a perspective of self-healing which enables the best results for her clients. This multiple perspective has inspired the *Practical Guide* series, of which this book is the third.

WHAT PEOPLE ARE SAYING

ADELAIDE GRIEF AND LOSS SUPPORT GROUP – (IN-PERSON)

"*After completing this course, I have become more in tune with how I was feeling, why and how to become once again a well-balanced person achieving happiness in life again and how to be realistic with my thoughts and feelings.*" L.V.R.

LILY COURSE: PLATINUM LEVEL—YOUR BEREAVEMENT JOURNEY (ONLINE PROGRAM)

"*The New Creations Grief Course came to me at the right time in my grief journey. I was fortunate to do the Lily Course and found it very helpful, practical, gentle, and reflective. It has given me some tangible tools and new insights to support me every day. Grief is hard; however, this course allows you to be kind to yourself whatever you are processing and continue to move forward.*" S.W.

DAISY COURSE: GOLD LEVEL - YOUR BEREAVEMENT JOURNEY (ONLINE PROGRAM)

"*I'm looking at the world a lot happier, feeling a lot more positive and not carrying the heavy load of grief. The hardest part was putting that first word on paper. Have had multiple losses over a relatively short time and 2 family members suddenly taken 17 years ago. Hadn't ever grieved properly. Seven losses which was a lot to put on paper.*

Thank you for all the work and the modules you have put together. It is well set out in the correct stages of the grief process. It worked for me. I can talk about the deceased to family and friends now without crying or carrying what felt like a 20 kgs of weight on my shoulders.

I'm more confident and stronger...I now notice I have a lot of positive supportive friends around me. I thought I was so alone before. Thank you once again. Also, a very positive comment in the tea-room from a lady. She doesn't know what I have been working through- said I looked great, had a glow about me and was happier and she said my smile gave it away.

Thank you". R.W.

SERVICES AND OPTIONS

To find out more information about me and the services I provide, go to www.dianahutchison.com

There is an option to book a FREE thirty-minute assessment call, via the 'Book Appointment' page on my website www.dianahutchison.com/book-appointment or through https://diana-hutchison.au3.cliniko.com/bookings

If you wish to add to your self-assessment, I have created a grief and loss checklist that may give you an idea whether you could benefit from professional input and support in your grief processing. This is a FREE checklist you can download from www.dianahutchison.com/shop

You can also check out my online programs for loss through death and for loss through other circumstances at www.newyoucreations.com

To find out about other titles in the 'Practical Guide' series, go to www.amazon.com/author/dianahutchison and follow me.

I would love it if you could please leave a review of any of my books you read and find empowering or helpful on your favourite platform.

COMING SOON

The fourth book in the Practical Guide series:

A Practical Guide for Healing Our World from The Inside Out

To learn more about what Diana offers for your self-healing please visit www.dianahutchison.com and sign up for her newsletter. To be updated on her upcoming books, you may follow her on Amazon at www.Amazon.com/author/dianahutchison

www.dianahutchison.com/shop